Notes & Apologies:

- ✯ Annual subscriptions to *The Believer* include four issues, one of which might be themed and may come with a special bonus item, such as a giant poster, free radio series, or annual calendar. View our subscription deals at *thebeliever.net/subscribe*.

- ✯ Dispersed throughout the issue is a microinterview with musician Dustin Payseur, conducted by our assistant editor, Bryce Woodcock. Payseur is the frontman of the Brooklyn, New York–based band Beach Fossils, which formed in 2009. The band has since released four full-length albums on Bayonet, a record label Payseur cofounded with his wife. Widely recognized as a pioneer of the lo-fi dream pop subgenre, Payseur spoke to Woodcock over the phone from his tiny soundproofed home studio after he'd just finished putting his daughter to bed.

- ✯ The incidental illustrations in this issue, of a woman in various states of readerly repose, are by Noémie Chust.

DEAR THE BELIEVER

849 VALENCIA STREET, SAN FRANCISCO, CA 94110

letters@thebeliever.net

Dear Believer,
I have come of age during the writer-as-influencer era, when making a living as a journalist seems to require not only producing good work, but also crafting a marketable personal brand. Often, this process of self-building is tied to consumption and self-improvement: writers tell us what they eat for breakfast, how they structure their days, what makeup they wear.

I was feeling suffocated trying to grow as a writer in this ecosystem, so I reflexively turned in the opposite direction, romanticizing those authors who seem to erase themselves from their work, like the pseudonymous Elena Ferrante, or this year's Nobel Prize in Literature laureate, Han Kang, who rejected a celebration banquet after her win because, she said, "I wanted to stay quiet. There's so much suffering in the world, and I believe we should respond more quietly."

I used to see their work as pure: art separated from the artist. Ross Simonini's "The Joy of Persona" (Winter 2024) complicated that understanding. Simonini distinguishes between "personality," which is "shaped by genetics and the vicissitudes of life," and "persona," which is "an invented, enhanced, and performed version of personality." Persona, he argues, isn't limited to what an artist wears or eats—it can also be created through their craft and style, what they share with an audience. "The boundaries of our persona are defined through an accumulation of choices," Simonini writes.

Persona persists even in works written from a distance: "If I hid my presence, as another writer might, the authorship would still be here, in my tone, in the movement of my thoughts, and even in what I refuse to reveal." Ferrante's decision to obscure her identity doesn't negate her persona—it's arguably her most persona-defining choice. Her interviews, correspondences, and lectures also shape her persona, one of a writer wrestling with the limits of language, who sees reality as a "whirlpool of debris" that cannot be captured fully in words. This persona provides context for craft and plot choices in her Neapolitan Quartet, from her restless, comma-spliced sentences, to the inexplicable burning of Lila's wedding-day portrait, which had been displayed in the Solaras' shop against her will. The outward-facing self that Ferrante has constructed across her fiction and nonfiction doesn't take away from her work; it enriches it.

Creating a persona, then, need not be a consumerist project popularized by the internet. Simonini offers a liberating alternative: persona as a work of art in itself.

Nina Pasquini
Somerville, MA

Dear Believer,
Regarding the embarrassing friend who speaks too loudly ("Ask Carrie," Fall 2024): I would like to respectfully suggest an alternative handling of that situation.

I come from a large family of loud talkers. We are not auctioneers or drill sergeants, and most of us do not particularly enjoy the situations in which we are inclined to talk loudly—we do not hear well! Background noise can make it virtually impossible to communicate or even to know how loudly we are speaking. I am surprised that this did not come up in your list of potential reasons for loud talking.

I feel sensitive about speaking too loudly, and very much appreciate a covert hand signal to remind me to reduce my volume. Treading lightly on this topic (or choosing loud destinations!?) will never get your Quieter Friend to a happy place with people like me! A good friend can get away with a plainly stated observation like "You speak louder than I do. Can you hear me, or should I try to speak louder too?" This sort of statement gives the loud friend an opportunity to mention her reasons, and perhaps even how she feels about speaking so loudly. Helpful hand signals could then be planned out.

This would be the best-case scenario for me, and would result in us choosing quieter destinations, not louder ones!

Terry Sullivan
Cincinnati, OH

THE **INDEX**
to issue one hundred forty-nine

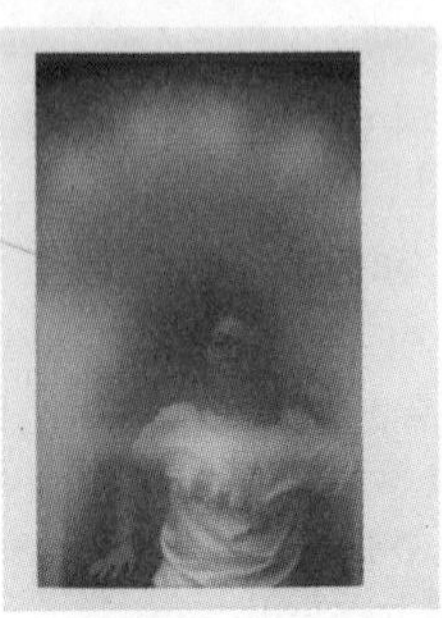

"BECAUSE IN THOSE MOMENTS WHEN YOU'RE IN PURSUIT OF SOMETHING, YOU HAVE A HEIGHTENED LEVEL OF CONSCIOUSNESS."
p. 49

THE BELIEVER: You mentioned that you've been working so hard since you were fifteen.
LISA LUCAS: I don't know if it was "so hard," but yes, working.
BLVR: But even the fact that you've dared to try different art forms: I'm very impressed by that.
LL: I'm getting a little old to be brave.

Compiled by Maya Segal and Lula Konner; portraits by Kristian Hammerstad; photo courtesy of Adalena Kavanagh

"YOU HAVE THE PARASITIC MONSTERS OF OUR ANIMAL PAST, AND THEN THIS AI FUTURE, AND THEY'RE BOTH TRYING TO KILL HUMANITY."

p. 27

Spot illustration by Noémie Chust; photo courtesy of Searchlight Pictures

THE ROUTINE: ARIA ABER

AN ANNOTATED RAMBLE THROUGH ONE ARTIST'S WORKDAY

9–11 a.m.

9 a.m.

Waking up and coffee. Looking for the cat. She's sleeping on her pillow under the bed, as always!

9:20 a.m.

It's the week between Christmas and New Year's, so everyone's gone. I have no meetings scheduled, the semester is over, the Pilates studio is closed, grading is done. I'm listening to *Democracy Now!* and scrolling the internet. Everything is horrible on all fronts.

11 a.m.–3 p.m.

11 a.m.

Responding to emails and WhatsApp messages from friends in Europe and calling my sister in Germany.

My kitchen table nook with the laptop. The window looks out on the roofs of adjacent buildings.

11:30 a.m.

How to live? Can't relax. Need to work. I turn off my email app and put my phone away. I'm revising and taking notes for my next project: a short story. Looking at declassified documents "for research."

3–7 p.m.

3 p.m.

Can't work. Need to move my body. I go on a walk around Prospect Park while listening to a podcast. I spy the boathouse.

Afternoon light falls on the door of the boathouse in Prospect Park.

4:20 p.m.

Working some more, which today means answering interview questions about *Good Girl* with the cat on my lap.

The cat is named Jeanie.

7 p.m.–12 a.m.

7 p.m.

My husband and I discuss what we want for dinner. We settle on cabbage and bean soup, so we need to go out for groceries.

7:45 p.m. → **8:30 p.m.**

Playing hide-and-seek with the cat.

Dinner!

9 p.m.

Reading the galley of Michael Clune's *Pan*, which is incredibly riveting.

Pan is about a young narrator suffering from panic attacks and his obsession with the god Pan.

12–3 a.m.

12 a.m.

My husband is going to sleep, and I'm back to working on my short story. Writing is just so much easier at night. This is when the magic happens.

2 a.m. → **2:30 a.m.**

Watching about ten to thirteen orca videos on my phone (guilty).

I crawl into bed and read some more.

3 a.m.

Sleep, at last. ★

Photographs by the author

ASK CARRIE

A QUARTERLY COLUMN FROM
CARRIE BROWNSTEIN, WHO IS BETTER
AT DISPENSING ADVICE THAN TAKING IT

Send questions to advice@thebeliever.net

Q: *About a year ago, my friend asked me to start sharing my real-time location with her. At first, the layer of forced transparency made me anxious. What if I want to reschedule our plans, but I'm just sitting at home? What if I'm running late because I can't figure out what to wear, and not because I'm stuck in traffic? But here I am a year later, getting ready to meet up with Location-Sharing Friend, and I'm the one who's abusing my power. I just checked her location to see how far away she is—a habit I've formed, and something I do even when we have no plans. She's five minutes away. What's your opinion on location sharing? Is it a sign of intimacy, or just downright invasive?*

—Ella M., Location not found

A: I don't mean to sound alarmist or paranoid, but I'm definitely going to. Location sharing is largely a scam and should be used sparingly. Such as in emergencies, or when you're headed into potential and—this is the crucial part—actual danger. Because otherwise, all you're doing is surrendering to surveillance capitalism, forfeiting autonomy, and weakening resilience. Ironically, many of us will fight for bodily and political autonomy, support safe spaces, respect privacy, and abhor trespass and violation, but are boundaryless when it comes to technology (even when it's the nefarious, untrustworthy sort), willingly making ourselves susceptible to manipulation and behavior modification at the hands of our devices. And while it might be too late to reverse this ontological shift, or the merging of the virtual and the actual, we must resist where we can. The more we allow our likes and habits, our bodies and minds, to be available and porous to tech, the more we cede not just control but awareness, a sense that it knows more about us than we know about ourselves. Tech isn't augmenting us, but the other way around.

And if that doesn't scare you, let me appeal on a more personal level. Location sharing with your friends forms nothing more than an illusory connection. It's the opposite of closeness, tethering people to their devices, not to one another. It's an example of tech gamifying personal dynamics: *My friend is a dot on a map that I can follow. I invent narratives based on their whereabouts, and judge accordingly. Higher value is placed on being in a certain place at a certain time. Being in the wrong place is a value deduction.* No wonder you are anxious! This relationship is now quantifiable and transactional, but moreover, it's exhausting! It's starting to make sense why everyone is in avoidance mode and canceling plans these days.

My advice for you is to stop sharing your location and start sharing the things that help maintain and nurture a friendship: your time; your capacity for

Illustration by Kristian Hammerstad

listening; your compassion, patience, and understanding.

As a sidenote: If I go missing, it's probably because this answer makes me a target of the Tech Overlords. Too bad there's no way to ensure that help could find me…

Q: *I met a friend online, and at first we really hit it off. But lately she's been crossing some boundaries. She's started reaching out to all my friends, trying to get close to them, and organizing events that always involve me—sometimes without even asking if I'm free. It's becoming overwhelming, and her voracious social appetite is a serious energy drain.*

I've never had to confront a friend about something like this before, but I need some breathing room. How do I set boundaries without hurting her feelings or making things awkward?

Selena E.
Seattle, WA

A: Setting boundaries is a difficult task, but I agree you need to set some guidelines with this friend. As opposed to, say, doing the easier thing, which is to break up with not just her but your entire friend group, so that you never have to see her again or confront the problem. Or maybe move cities entirely. While I'm sure you've thought about doing both, I'm confident you can ask for breathing room without jeopardizing your friendship.

Here's what to do: Be kind but firm, use clear and concise language, and above all else, don't apologize for asking for what you need. Start with what you like and appreciate about her as a friend. Then tell her your needs, plain and simple, without hedging or qualifying. Explain what a balanced friendship feels like to you, and ask what she looks for in a friend. Perhaps through the process of clarification and transparency, she'll understand why you've been uncomfortable, and you'll gain a better understanding of her actions. She might be operating out of insecurity and not maliciousness, but she needs to see how it looks from your end. Additionally—and maybe this is the hard part—accept that her feelings might get hurt. (I suspect it's thinking we're responsible for everyone else's feelings that makes boundary setting difficult in the first place.) So allow for her feelings, and don't try to mollify them in the moment. Her anger, confusion, discomfort, whatever it may be, is temporary.

Even if she doesn't do so immediately, I think she'll appreciate the honesty. If she isn't able to accept your needs, I hear Boise, Idaho, is nice.

Q: *Everyone says I'm lucky to look young, but it often works against me professionally and socially. As an adjunct professor, I moonlighted at a college bar where coworkers treated me like a student until they realized I was their age. I'm always the only one carded when I go out with colleagues, and at conferences I get comments that imply my inexperience, referencing the vast opportunities before me.* Buddy, you're like two years older than I am. We're at the same stage in our careers.

These episodes are usually good for a laugh, but the larger pattern is starting to grate on me—and constantly brushing it off gives people tacit permission to treat me in a diminutive way. How do I address this without coming off as overly sensitive?

Baby-Faced Professional
Houston, TX

MICROINTERVIEW WITH DUSTIN PAYSEUR, PART I

THE BELIEVER: Beach Fossils has been officially active for over fifteen years. How would you describe the original impetus behind the band's sound?

DUSTIN PAYSEUR: At first, the idea for the project was to do one specific sound with really specific influences. I was challenging myself to do something that was more focused, because I'm so ADHD—I always have been. In all my musical projects before I started Beach Fossils, every song sounded like it was from a completely different genre. When I started sending demos out to labels, I was like, This is just too all-over-the-place to make sense to anybody. So I tried to focus on a sound. I had the things that were influencing me at the time, which was mostly '80s UK indie rock, and I started pulling from those and post-punk and seeing where I could take the sound. Somehow I was able to get away with not completely ripping that stuff off. I added my own spin to it—which I think is hard, but at the time I wasn't even doing it on purpose. ★

A: Everyone is right: you are lucky. But I imagine it's also difficult to be perpetually underestimated, so I empathize with your plight. I'll call the condition with which you are afflicted the Ronan Farrow Syndrome, wherein one's cherubic face sets off a cognitive dissonance in others, resulting in confusion, mistrust, and skepticism. Fortunately, there are ways to manage your RFS, the first being a beard, real or fake, no matter your gender. Don't be afraid to make this facial hair gray, something that conjures Father Time but still manages to be chic. Second, let people know how dry your skin feels. No, really: Talk about it. Use excessive amounts of hand lotion and lip balm. Have these on or close to you at all times by placing them everywhere: near the front door, in a pocket of every coat you own, in your car, in your favorite backpack. Discover a ChapStick you didn't know you'd put somewhere. You'll be surprised by how elated you feel when you happen upon the small container; it will have been a while since joy has overtaken you like this. Next, add sighing to your repertoire. Not in response to anything or anyone specific, simply because. Like exercise, or in place of it, it's nice to have a routine. The louder and longer the sigh, the better, and never sit or rise without one.

I can almost guarantee that making these small adjustments to your appearance and routine will convey not only maturity but senescence. I must caution you, however, that there's only one proven cure for RFS, and that is time. Eventually, Baby-Faced Professional, you will not just be old, you'll look old, or at least older. Still youthful, perhaps, but not young. At which point you'll long for the days of being carded at bars and mistaken for a college student.

Q: *It's my first winter in the Pacific Northwest, and the unending damp, gray, and cold are starting to get to me. Any advice to combat seasonal depression?*

Greg F.
Portland, OR

A: As a lifelong Pacific Northwesterner, I relate to your struggles. Though I've yet to try one, medical professionals often tout the proven benefits of a light therapy box for seasonal affective disorder (SAD). So I'd be remiss if I didn't pass that advice on to you. As for me, here's how I usually cope: I wear a coat and knit hat in the house to counter the damp, bone-chilling cold. If other people in your home aren't asking if you're about to head out, you're doing it wrong. I also drink hot tea throughout the day. Chamomile, mint, or an herbal blend that promises the same effect as pills. While coffee is wonderful in the morning, you want to avoid drinking too much caffeine. After all, sleep is when you can shut out the misery, and it's not to be jeopardized. Additionally, I set a reading or movie-watching goal for the winter. Pick an author or subject, director, genre, or actor, and create a list of books or films. Make it a reasonable number, something achievable; goal-setting helps counter the shapelessness of the dreary days, and the way gray skies melt time. Productivity is less about getting shit done and more about imposing an architecture on the void. This year I'm reading books about the Vietnam War, which means I've entered the military history phase of my life, an indication that by next year I'll be building model planes. Um. I'll be honest, Greg: As I write this, I'm less and less sure I'm combatting my own seasonal depression. What I've described is a woman sitting around her house in outerwear, mug of tea in mittened hand, reading about war. Maybe it's time to purchase that SAD lamp. ✭

MICROINTERVIEW WITH DUSTIN PAYSEUR, PART II

THE BELIEVER: You're a very eclectic listener, but Beach Fossils has maintained a relatively focused sound. How much intention goes into maintaining an aesthetic through line despite all the styles of music you listen to?

DUSTIN PAYSEUR: Honestly, I see that less as a positive and more as a curse. I am inspired by so many different things, but I do have a project that is generally, you know, "a thing." It's a thing that you can expect when you put on an old song or a new song. I would honestly love to experiment with more genres and styles, but when I sit down to work on music, I try not to think too much about what's going to happen. ✭

CLOSE READ

UNPACKING ONE REDOUBTABLE PASSAGE.

IN THIS ISSUE: *THE CHILDREN'S CRUSADE* [1] BY MARCEL SCHWOB, TRANSLATED BY KIT SCHLUTER

by Chris Molnar

THE THREE LITTLE CHILDREN'S TALE

The three of us, Nicolas [2] who knows not how to speak, Alain, and Denis, we set out on the roads to go to Jerusalem. [3] We have been walking a long time. [4] There were white voices [5] calling to us in the night. They called to all the little children. They were like the voices of birds dead in the winter. [6] And at first we saw many poor birds lying on the frozen earth, many little red-throated birds. Then we saw the first flowers and the first leaves and we wove them into crosses. [7] We sang before the villages, as we used to [8] for the New Year. And all the children ran to us. And we went forth like a flock. There were men who cursed us, knowing not the Lord. There were women who held us back by the arms and questioned us, and covered our faces with kisses. And then there were the kind souls who brought us wooden bowls, of warm milk and fruit. [9] And everyone pitied us. For they know not where we are going and have not heard the voices.

On the land are thick forests, and rivers, and mountains, and paths full of bramble. And at the end of the land lies the sea we are soon to cross. And at the end of

27

(1) First published in France in 1896, *The Children's Crusade* is Marcel Schwob's fictional study of the real-life Children's Crusade, an early thirteenth-century European young person's religious revival. Later, Schwob anthologized the work with *Mimes* (1893), *The Book of Monelle* (1894), and *The Wooden Star* (1897) in a collection called *La lampe de Psyché* (Psyche's lamp) (1903), which gathered his writings on childhood. The straightforward psychedelic wonder of childhood and the figure of the wandering urchin are constants in his work, implicitly connected to the source of creativity and the positive energy of life.

(2) Although the Children's Crusade is said to have had a leader named Nicholas, a young shepherd from the Rhineland, Schwob's children seem to be French and are merely guileless followers. As history would have it—though Schwob's version leaves this out too—the French children were led by another shepherd, twelve years old, named Stephen.

(3) Jerusalem had by this time (roughly 1212) been conquered by the Ayyubid Sultanate, though rump Crusader states persisted along the Syrian coastline. There is still disagreement about whether those failing imperial projects and faraway harbingers of Western doom influenced the movements of children in Europe, or if tales of the Children's Crusade have been compiled from unrelated religious revivals.

(4) Translator Kit Schluter recalls the necessity of keeping this chapter, one of the only ones in the novel told from the perspective of the children, in "as naïve a voice as possible."

(5) The "voix blanche" (white voice) can mean "a toneless voice" in French, or, in the more current argot, a plaintive, open-throated folk singing. Here, Schwob uses the phrase to allude to winter and the supernatural. This kind of subtle estrangement is crucial to how his historical tales become fugues and myths.

(6) Schwob's comparison of ghostly voices to those of dead birds immediately transitions to a concrete vision of dead birds, red throats connoting both the color of life and a slash of death. This depth of wordplay ties him to the symbolists, while pointing forward to the surrealists; the meanings are clear yet slip into the beyond.

(7) In his introduction to the book, Jorge Luis Borges quotes the obscure French writer René Lalou on "the 'sober precision' with which Schwob has related the 'naïve legend,'" saying that "this precision does not render it any less legendary or pathetic. Did Gibbon not observe that the pathetic tends to arise from trivial circumstances?" The weaving of crosses has the children unconsciously, playfully building a religious symbol of death, perhaps their own.

(8) In the only other widely available English translation, by Henry Copley Greene from 1898, the children sing as they are "wont to do," which misses the plangent sense of the past in the original's "ainsi que nous avions coutume."

(9) The Children's Crusade ended, as legend has it, with the children lost, or sold into slavery in southern Europe, after being impelled to march impossibly toward Jerusalem, having been told that the Mediterranean Sea would part. By eliding the tragedy, and instead writing of the ephemeral charity of strangers, Schwob emphasizes the universal poignancy of warm, passing moments. ★

RESURRECTOR

A ROTATING GUEST COLUMN IN WHICH WRITERS REEXAMINE CRITICALLY UNACCLAIMED WORKS OF ART. IN THIS ISSUE: "LIKE A G6."

by Chris Gayomali

In my mid-twenties, most Fridays after work, I would frequent Asian-themed nights at clubs like White Rabbit in the Lower East Side, mostly because the drinks were cheap and the girl I had a crush on was going to be there. The dance floor was always a little sticky, and it wasn't unusual to go home at 4 a.m. with someone's rogue eyelash smushed into your shoe.

Those Friday nights more or less defined one of the weirder transition periods of my adult life—new to New York City; terminally broke; wearing cheap, wrinkle-free work shirts from H&M that probably osmosed microplastics into my bloodstream—yet I remember developing something of a personal ritual whenever the DJ played the song "Like a G6" by Far East Movement, which was everywhere at the time: I'd go outside and smoke a cigarette.

Lest there be any confusion, this was mostly because I was young and stupid and filled with gloomy malaise. Back then, the song occupied a place in my subconscious, lying in proximity to other party anthems like "Let's Get It Started" by the Black Eyed Peas (sanitized from the original version, "Let's Get Retarded") and "Dynamite" by Taio Cruz. Spiritually, "G6" inspired a mild existential spiral in me every time those first few synths caused the floor to wobble, a stark reminder that I was spending eight hours a day sitting

at a desk job I loathed, and the only antidote was two-for-one vodka sodas served with too much ice.

The song went to number one on the Billboard pop charts, which was unheard of for an Asian group at the time, especially pre–"Gangnam Style," pre-BTS. But even at the top of the music world, Far East Movement went largely ignored by the elite players in music media. (Which, in a way, is kind of a fundamental part of the Asian American experience.) *Pitchfork* didn't bother to review their album *Free Wired*, while *Rolling Stone* said that it was "music designed to make two-year-olds deliriously giddy." Plenty of music bloggers abhorred it too. One of the meaner-spirited reviews noted that there are "bad songs out there, and then there's 'Like a G6.' It's as if someone found Ke$ha's Asian-American extended family, got them trashed on absinthe laced with meth, guided them to a MacBook with GarageBand, told them to write a song that sounds dated already, and put the results on the radio."

Time, though, has a haloing effect, which is why I've since come to appreciate, even love, "Like a G6" like no other guilty pleasure in my life: more than "Post to Be," "Faithfully," and anything by Skrillex. It's just so damn good. Transcendent, in fact. I like to imagine that "Like a G6" is what they play in the seventh ascension of the Galaxy Brain, a tesseract where linear time ceases to exist and the past and future become one.

Part of my initial resistance to the song, I think, was that, as a New York transplant, I was experiencing a latent form of shame about having grown up around Los Angeles, where the foursome were also from. They were having fun, being stupid, going dumb. I mostly wasn't; I was trying to look smart. I thought of them as over-the-top characters, loud and unapologetic in their big indoor sunglasses and bow ties and high-top sneakers paired with skinny jeans. They were Kev Nish (Kevin Nishimura), Prohgress (James Roh), J-Splif (Jae Choung), and DJ Virman (Virman Coquia)—a Japanese Chinese American, two Korean Americans, and a Filipino American. As far as California Asian friend-group compositions go, Far East Movement was basically my homie group chat.

The song is a study in contrasts—brute maximalism on the surface with an undercurrent of restraint. Its structure is deceptively minimal: a chorus

Illustration by Derick Jones

that's repeated four times (with lyrics borrowed from a Dev track called "Booty Bounce"), a zippy pre-chorus, and verses so simple and monotonous that they sound like incantations for spells. But the thing that actually makes the song *hard* is how scrappy it is. The melody was a happy accident; as Niles Hollowell-Dhar, a.k.a. KSHMR—who produced the song as one half of the Cataracs—explained in 2012. After he mistakenly dragged a high-pitched bell into the wrong lane of his production software, those crunchy first few bars of synthesizer—the *dun-dun-duns*—were born.

Necessity being the mother of invention and whatnot, the song also pushed forward new internal rhyme schemes (*blizzard* with *slizzard* and *sizzurp*); new luxury airplanes (the group didn't even realize that the G650 was a real plane at the time; they were inspired to "make up" the G6 after Drake rapped about knowing "G4 pilots on a first-name basis" in the posse track "Forever"); and new places for Asian Americans to occupy in the collective consciousness.

The foursome knew they had something special in their hands when they first heard the Cataracs beat back in 2008. But it would be another eighteen months before they actually finished writing the song, and not for lack of trying.

What took so long? Well, as they tell it, they made the perfectly understandable mistake of trying to *rap* over the beat: to write lyrics that meant something. "We came from spoken word and all this other stuff," Nishimura told me, when I met the group on a Zoom call recently. "But we've been in the clubs enough to know that, especially in the 2010 era, if it's too wordy, the DJ is not playing it. They're playing Lil Jon. They're playing all this crunk stuff."

So the group went dumb, then dumber, then dumbest—i.e., rhyming *Three 6* with *G6*—until the song was stripped to its essential components. Pure id. Ultra instinct. As with all enduring works of art, "Like a G6" is a product of relentless self-editing, a paring down that would make Strunk and White proud. (I'd also argue that one of the song's brightest spots is the elegant inversion of the typical club trope where drunk groupies are treated like some sort of weird prize: "Sober girls around me, / they be actin' like they drunk.") The group says the song was a pretty faithful representation of their lives back then too. "I don't feel like we were even being loud versions of ourselves," said Roh. "That's who we were, bro! We were club rats. The only difference is the girls we were hanging out with might not have been as hot as the girls in the video."

In some ways, it's easy to trace the through line from "Like a G6" to *Crazy Rich Asians*, to the record label 88rising, to a Marvel franchise about a C-tier superhero who happens to be Chinese. (While researching this essay, I was lightly shocked that the song was never actually in a *Fast & Furious* movie—my own personal Mandela effect.) I'm not saying "G6" made all that other stuff possible, but it did open the door, just a crack, for Asian diasporic art to be crude, silly, and maybe even a little obnoxious. Sometimes you fly high so there's less resistance. ✭

MICROINTERVIEW WITH DUSTIN PAYSEUR, PART III

THE BELIEVER: How do you approach writing lyrics that are focused and deeply personal to your own experience, while also trying to connect with a broader audience?

DUSTIN PAYSEUR: I've found that the more specific I get, the more people connect with it. At first I thought I had to keep my lyrics vague because otherwise people wouldn't connect. But I couldn't help but start writing more and more specifically, and people were like, *I know exactly what you're talking about.*

BLVR: That reminds me of something you said about being inspired by New York School poets. People like Frank O'Hara, Ted Berrigan, and Anne Waldman.

DP: I was reading Ted Berrigan almost every day while I was writing the lyrics for *Bunny*. That stuff is so real that it just never feels dated. You could pick up a book like that from the '50s, and as long as they're talking like a regular person and they're being vulnerable, disturbingly explicit, you're like, Wow, this is how people have always felt. ✭

WHAT DOES THE AURACAMERA 6000 SEE?

THREE VISITS TO MAGIC JEWELRY, A SMALL SHOP IN MANHATTAN'S CHINATOWN WHERE SPECTRAL PHOTOGRAPHS REVEAL SOMETHING MORE THAN AURA COLOR

by Adalena Kavanagh

Today we live in the Great Vibes epoch. Inherent yet ephemeral, vibes are difficult to measure. They're the perfect concept for a period when "if you know, you know" is answer enough. Uncertainty is the fraught space where pseudo-prophetic practices like aura photography thrive. Still, who doesn't want promises of self-knowledge, healing, and growth when we know what the problems are but change seems futile?

Last summer I visited Magic Jewelry's two locations in Manhattan's Chinatown, which specialize in feng shui, healing crystals, and aura photography. Display cases at both shops were crammed with crystals, stones, and various talismans related to Buddhism and other Chinese religions. In the window of the Elizabeth Street store is a classic feng shui protective talisman, a Later Heaven bagua. This octagonal mirror is a feng shui energy map, and it sits on a fabric background embroidered with flowers and dragons. On top of the bagua sit eight dark, ferocious stone frogs (thought to attract wealth) surrounding a clear crystal that to me looks like a smiling lion or goofy-faced deity. The object is labeled in Chinese as 財源滾滾—cáiyuángǔngǔn, which means "profits pouring in from all sides," or, as my dictionary puts it, "raking in money."

During my visit to the Centre Street location, I was led to a corner and told to place my hands on two blue boxes with metal hand-shaped contacts connected to another blue metal box. This was the AuraCamera 6000, a machine created and marketed by Guy Coggins in the 1970s. My first reader didn't allow any photographs, claiming it was company policy. She was an older Chinese woman, and my mother is Taiwanese, so when she began my reading I stood up straighter, feeling the only judgment that can truly wound me: that of a slightly disapproving older Asian woman. She said I was intuitive and a thinker who tries to do the right thing. As the photograph developed, she complimented the brightness of my aura—in the photo I can barely be made out; the only visible part of my body is my face. A bright white light is right above my head. Above that is another sweep of light, like colored balls that shift from pink to green to blue.

She pulled out a chart that explained the *chakras*, a Sanskrit word that can be translated as "cycles." These focal points of energy are believed to be spinning wheels that life energy flows through, similar to how qi flows through meridians. The chakras are located along the spine, from the crown chakra, at the top of the head, down through the brow chakra (a.k.a. the third eye), throat chakra, heart chakra, solar plexus chakra, navel chakra, and finally the root or base chakra. In the photo, an aqua light surrounds my heart chakra; below, the light around my soft belly is pinkish-purple. As she droned on, my mind strayed to articles I'd read about people sunning their yonis. I widened my eyes so my skepticism wasn't too obvious.

When she asked if I'd been busy recently, I made a tight-lipped concession to that fact. For the upcoming academic year, I would be on sabbatical from the school library I manage, and I was making preparations for my absence. She pointed to my shoulder and said I had tightness on my right side, then touched my midsection in the photo and diagnosed inflammation in my stomach. She advised me to get more sleep, eat earlier, and eat less—all admonitions my mother makes, and which I mostly ignore.

The second time I visited, I got a similar reading, albeit with more effusive praise. "Wah, so pretty!" my reader exclaimed, upon looking at my photo. My aura this time was bright green with some yellow, instead of white and

Photographs throughout courtesy of the author

purplish. She said green means changes, a new job or project. "Also, green means money," she said with a laugh, adding, "Money is easy come, easy go."

Again I thought of my mother. After a recent move to the Bronx, my mom had babied her green "money plant," cooing to it, "I know you miss your brothers and sisters in Brooklyn, but you can grow strong here." Then she assured me the plant was now robust, "making money grow" for her and my father. A few weeks later, my father hit a Lotto jackpot for the second time this year. The first time he hit it, he'd played the first three numbers of my birthdate and used the money to fund my parents' move. For the second winning jackpot, he played those same numbers backward. That money is going toward rent.

Once again, my reader suggested I sleep more, avoid eating late at night, and eat less. Then she tried to sell me some crystals as cures: black obsidian, citrine, and amethyst. She pointed out the "crystal chair": a simple folding chair underneath what looked like a palanquin straight out of a Chinese historical drama. The wooden frame had a triangular brass bell roof, from which hung strings of clear crystals. She said many people come sit there to cleanse their energy. I left without giving it a try. I promised I'd be back to buy some crystals.

The technology of aura photography has its roots in a technique developed back in 1939 by Russian scientists Semyon and Valentina Kirlian, who generated phantasmal effects by connecting a high-voltage source to a photographic plate. Kirlian photography was seen for decades as a potential diagnostic tool for health, and perhaps this is what gives it the illusion of impartiality. Today, as you look at your aura, a reader dispenses personalized attention: confirming your desires, validating your ailments. Tangible proof comes in the form of the photograph.

Looking at all the green in my second photo, a wide band going from the right (the past) to the left (the future) gave me some hope for the prospects of my novel, which is on submission. Alas, the photos themselves were disappointing: in previous years, aura readers used a now discontinued film that had higher fidelity, and the photography purist in me longed for that era. Then I recalled that whenever I'd walked by Magic Jewelry in the past, I'd always seen pairs of people leaving with their new mementos. They had someone who could tell them what they

A LOOSE GUIDE TO AURA READING
(NOT APPLICABLE TO CHILDREN)

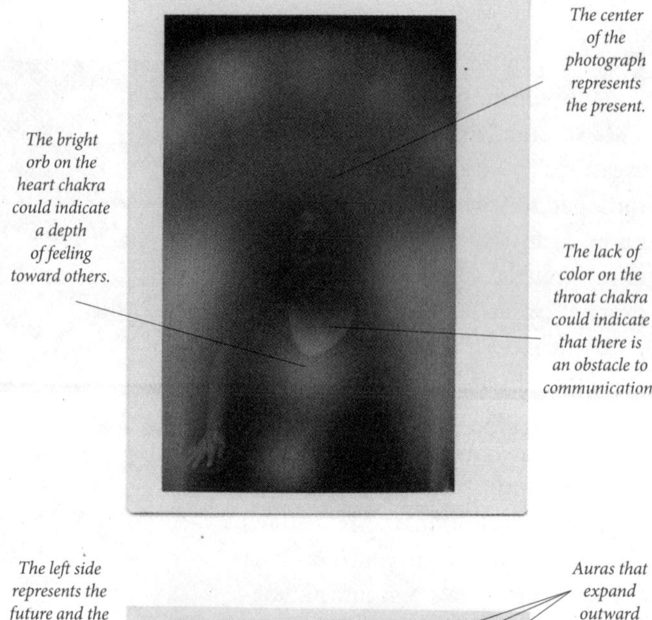

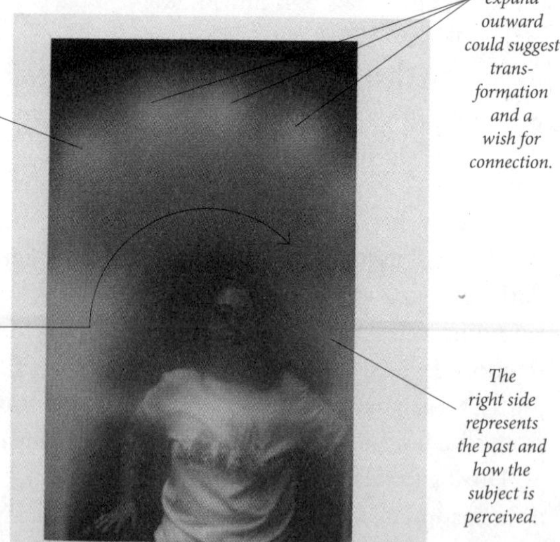

RED	ORANGE	YELLOW	GREEN	BLUE	PURPLE	WHITE
Passion, restlessness, power	Liveliness, sociability, sensuality	Optimism, joy, generosity	Healing, patience, growth	Creativity, devotion, honesty	Intuitiveness, empathy, spirituality	Transcendence, humility, cosmic wisdom

looked like while the reader was explaining their aura. They had someone to share the experience with, not just the object in their hands.

For my third aura reading, Nadia, the same reader I'd had the second time, was joined by an assistant who offered me a cup of hot green tea. When the assistant sat me down, she asked in Chinese if I speak Chinese. I said, "Yidian dian," which means "a little bit" in Mandarin, but when I say it, it means "I am greatly saddened and ashamed that I no longer do."

Nadia has been reading auras for thirty years and is from Taiwan, near my mother's hometown. Once she learned of our shared heritage, she was just as solicitous as the last time, but less impersonal. She said this third photo was very different from my first two. My colors were more indigo and purple, and the image was sharper, meaning I was more at peace, while still being sensitive to other people's perceptions. She said I treat people with kindness but sometimes I put distance between myself and others to give myself space. When she asked if that was correct, I didn't want to admit how apt it was. She told me not to overthink things and to go with my first instincts. She didn't tell me to eat less, or eat earlier, but again she said I should sleep more.

After my reading I asked about the crystal chair, and she invited me to sit in it. She told me to place my left hand on the large, clear crystal sphere and my right hand on the jagged black crystal, and then let their energy wash over me. I sat in the crystal chair while Nadia and her assistant attended to two other customers. While observing the room, I kept a private mantra going in my head about selling my book and maintaining stability in my relationship. The jagged crystal dug into my hand. I felt at peace, but between the scent of incense and all the wooden furniture around me, I thought the sense of peace wasn't really about my hopeful mantra and the energy crystals, but more about the fact that the shop resembled my Taiwanese grandmother's living room. It was neat but cluttered. To my right, next to the crystal chair, was a packaged hot oat drink with goji berries and a red bag of paper cups; to my left were Amway boxes with handwritten labels in Chinese. I watched the assistant help a thirtysomething woman carefully select beads for a bracelet. The woman's left hand was deformed. The other customer was a round-faced older woman with impeccable makeup and a confident smile. She was having a necklace restrung, and Nadia supplemented her passable Cantonese with "Okay-lah?," which in Cantonese has multiple intonations with varying meanings. I wanted to stay awhile longer, but soon Nadia asked if I was paying with cash or card.

Back in May, a few months before my first aura photo, I had stood in line at the annual Passport to Taiwan Festival in New York's Union Square to ask Mazu, Goddess of the Sea, if I would sell my novel. I appreciated the curtness with which the temple intermediary declared her answer, a brisk shake of the head: No. This shook me out of my impatience with the process, and I reassured myself that divination wasn't real. But when I walked into Magic Jewelry, the part of me susceptible to magical thinking hoped for the best. We all want someone to tell us that our dreams can still come true. ✯

QUEER LIBERATION
from DEEP FAKE

by Christopher Soto

Bought a T-shirt with Sylvia Rivera's face
Spent $50 to hear heterosexuals sing at Pride
Walked quickly past the unhoused
Clutching my Telfar leaving my Tesla
I'm not a capitalist just look at this mustache
Touch on these muscles while I read Judith Butler
I tell you Pride was a riot started in New York in 1969
Even though PRIDE was a collective in Los Angeles that
Protested police brutality outside the Black Cat Tavern in 1967
Too many people are worried about their irrelevance
I'm just worried about how my ass looks on Insta
I mean ending poverty and prisons at my nonprofit
Today I feel more like a brand than a person
Sometimes I wish Marsha P Johnson could spit on these gays
Then I wonder if she would spit on me too
Sometimes I want her spit on me to go viral
But not like that

16

A NEW POEM

by Ocean Vuong

I was a goner, they said. Oh
well. Could've been worse.
Could've been born
before they dug up
all the words. & we'd just stand
around trying not to
explode. I wanted,
above all, & with no
regard for human life, to play my Atari
& be alone without ugliness.
I admit I liked people best when
they're far away inside
me. Like on the phone
in the 90s. Could've
been worse. Could've
forgotten to invent scented markers
on purpose. The truth is, as
president, I was kind of a
walk-on. Most people hated
my guts. Others envied my
insane tallness. So I rubbed it in
by wearing the most obnoxious
hat ever made. I should've
worn it that night—but the war
was over &, like you, you bastard,
I was full of hope & liquid
dreams. Way back, before
the locomotive, I was actually
pretty, girlish even. But I aged 1,000 fucking years
in 3 winters just to show you
what it takes. To be the leader of endless
cannons. Asking fucked up
questions around fucked up
gentlemen. I was
the president of a place
melting away & never there, over
the bones of mothers
I can no longer
imagine. My liver's shit
& consumption's up there
in these parts. Most days I envy
the captain of the Titanic. I won't
explain. I've been walking
all night through this two
-stoplight town, my hat held behind me
like the softest, regrettable
turtle shell. I dropped my inhaler
back at the Dairy Queen &
didn't even look back. Doctor said
I don't need it but gave me one anyway
after Gettysburg. I'm sorry. I know
I didn't get here soon enough. But
history, too, is a cage. The bars
only becoming doors when you're
slipping thru as a ghost. Passing
the slaughter house, after the
YMCA, I covered my ears, even
if all I heard from the broken
windows were crickets going
crazy for sounding larger
than they were small. The hole
is no longer in my head—though
it's larger, somehow, in my
mind. There's a song kinda
stuck there, widening as I
talk. I'm always talking, Mary says,
dead. But tell me, how do we
fill it? The hole in God's green
heart, the marriage, the boys sleeping
in the dew with their fists tight
as roots, even the hole in the word
whole (sorry not sorry). Is it wrong, so
wrong, that I wished, above all, as a man,
to punch the sunflower in the face
just for having a face? I do
forgive McClellan his lack
of conviction. But more so,
I forgive Burnside. Poor

Burnside, too scared to be
brave & too brave to
be smart. Like the best
poets. Someone once said
a president is a kind of
pornographer. We make
the bodies buckle in
the halogen just to show
the world all that wanting
leads to a quiet so total
it makes Daguerreotypes
weep. Daguerre, Daguerre, of war,
of war, of war. Weren't there
other ways of singing? Was
anyone ever born? The thing
about the young & the very old
is they're both closest to
nothing. Oh, to be the president
of nothing! If only! To make
a grand speech full of anaphora
under a palm tree at the end
of the mind! Look, you people
know more about my war than
I ever did—& it's not fair. You didn't
sit up all night stroking their dusky
forehands & lighting the lamps.
All I wanted was
to carry my boy thru the snow
to that one hearth buried in
the armpit of the world &
forget. But a ghost, friends,
is not so bad. It's a ball of pain
just without the ball. Kinda like
a person—but only their shrug.
My wish, above all, was to be
so human, other humans, seeing
me crumpled on the floor, would
forgive their fathers. Forgive the finless sperm
who only knew one way. For
failing, always failing, to stop
the August ice cream from
melting on their fingers. For
waking up in a graveyard
after the quinceañera, hung over, only
to realize the graveyard is your
country & the blood on
your boots was always
your brother's. But all I did, after
walking from Washington,
was arrive at this federal
Ferris wheel. I touch the cold
beams, the femur of some
ancient Leviathan, & get on. I sit
waiting for the stars to change
knowing only their names will.
Shhh, it's starting. I can't
see them but hear the seats creaking
one by one. They're getting on
as the big wheel turns with
the weight of what's missing, the light
from that Citgo winking
over peeling steel. & I call out their names.
Robert! I say. Mary! Willie!
Thomas! Trevor! I say. Noah!
Lan! Phuong! Linh! Ma! Cau, oi!
& the giant clanks into motion.
Shhh—look at me, son. Despite
your faith in my near-sighted, limp
-wristed two-step, I was never
your president. I'm a sixteen
-year-old soul sack riding shotgun
on a haunted Ferris wheel
at the tri-county fair. Because the hole
in my skull is full of people. & these
people leaking from my dreams—
Lord, they are everything, everything
I had to give.

PLACE

THE HOME DEPOT

by Simon Wu

FEATURES:
- ☆ Ceiling fans
- ☆ Nursery
- ☆ Sheer and unrelenting possibility

I thought we had come to the Home Depot to replace the metal numbers on my mother's mailbox. But the problem we bring is not the problem we leave with. We walk down an aisle full of toilets, sinks, and light switches. Inexplicably, we are soon considering a patio repaving. And then new carpet for my brother's bedroom, and a garage conversion. At the Home Depot, home improvement dreams begin to look like a matter of elbow grease and the right YouTube video.

We are in Fairless Hills, Pennsylvania, at the location closest to my parents' house. As with many Home Depot stores, getting here is convenient if you have a car—I-295 and US Route 1 south will drop you off at its doorstep—but if you don't, good luck. The area is blighted with three-lane highways meant to ferry you exclusively between Chik-fil-A, the Oxford Valley Mall, BJ's, Sesame Place, and the suburbs.

We linger in the lighting aisle. It is easy to overlook the surreality of the Home Depot warehouse, where the components of a home have been dissected, taxonomized, and put on display. I look up at forty fans and chandeliers suspended from the ceiling, turned on for our comparative viewing pleasure. A house and a home are not the same, but under the ungodly glow of light fixtures for forty different houses, I can imagine one for our home.

I try to talk my mother out of the repaving, as it seems beyond her physical capabilities, given that she has just had knee-replacement surgery. But I realize that to think practically is to misunderstand the Home Depot's appeal. This place is about fantasy. And unlike IKEA, where the fantasy is pre-dreamed for you, Home Depot implores you to think bigger. What it lacks in editorial direction, it makes up for in sheer and unrelenting possibility.

Yet the Home Depot is also stubbornly real: home improvement quickly becomes bogged down by the particularities of hex bolts versus carriage bolts, or the appropriate type of caulk needed to seal gaps in your windows. Everything is harder to do than you think it is.

But actually some things are easier to do than you'd think! This is what my mom believes, at least. In the past, buoyed by the dreams of change, my mother and I have, with the help of the Home Depot, installed a new butcher-block counter; repainted her bedroom, and mine; resurfaced the kitchen cabinetry; created a shelving system for the laundry room; replaced the flooring in our covered patio; revitalized a dying garden bed; and evicted a groundhog from beneath a shed.

We emerge from the dark, sawdusty warehouse into my favorite part of the store: the tranquil open air of the Home Depot's nursery. Here we learn that nature's elements—soil, stones, plants—come in near-infinite, branded varieties. If you are looking, for example, to repave your patio, as we seem to be, again, you will find not only brick pavers, but also Gravalock, Techno Earth, Wellco, and VEVOR synthetic grid systems. Nearby, a squadron of garden fountains trickles water in a tsunami of Zen, and my mom asks an attendant the difference between gardening soil, houseplant soil, and organic soil: "Isn't it all just dirt?"

I wait by the mums and watch the sliding door into the warehouse open and close. When we were young, my mom used to bring me and my brothers to the Home Depot for free crafts workshops. We would ice skate with our sneakers on the sawdust floors. With soft mallets and Elmer's glue, we built birdhouses, storage boxes, and little trains. We wrote our names on the complimentary orange aprons, and the Sharpie bled through the thin fabric. All these things are still at my parents' place. If you look carefully, next to the laundry-room shelves, in a box sitting on the laminate flooring we installed twenty years ago, you'll find three mini birdhouses, shoddily constructed, lovingly preserved. ☆

Illustration by Kyle Hilton

NOAH HAWLEY

[FILMMAKER, WRITER]

INTERVIEWED BY—

JASON SCHWARTZMAN

[ACTOR, MUSICIAN]

"MY FAVORITE MOMENT IN PRODUCTION IS WALKING ON SET FOR THE FIRST TIME AND THINKING, THIS COULD GO HORRIBLY. BECAUSE THEN YOU'RE REALLY RISKING SOMETHING."

Some of Noah Hawley's thoughts on the original *Alien*:
It's blue-collar
It's almost like Waiting for Godot *in space*
It's all about not getting paid

Before Noah Hawley created his renowned television adaptation of the 1996 Coen brothers' classic film Fargo, *he spent most of his time writing novels. His first,* A Conspiracy of Tall Men *(1998), is about a professor of conspiracy theories who becomes embroiled in a mystery of his own when his wife dies in a plane bombing. As he plummets down one of the rabbit holes he has made a career of circling, the professor finally has good reason to be paranoid—only now he can't get his usual enjoyment from it. This predicament is typical of Hawley's work: respectable American life becomes a comic nightmare, and sanctioned pleasures turn perverse. But for Hawley, darkness need not mean doom. His magisterial command of plot—and of what makes it compulsive—is coupled with a remarkable gift for finding humor and goodness in stories of inexhaustible violence.*

Illustrations by Kristian Hammerstad

Born in New York City in 1967 to a family of writers, Hawley studied political science at Sarah Lawrence College and shortly thereafter began writing fiction while working as a paralegal, first in New York and later in San Francisco, where he also joined the Bay Area collective the Writers Grotto. On the heels of the publication of his debut novel, Hawley wrote and then sold his first screenplay, which would become the film Lies and Alibis. *This occurred during an auspicious six-month period when he also had his novel optioned by Paramount, and successfully pitched an idea for another movie. In the decades since, Hawley has written five novels; cowritten and directed the feature film* Lucy in the Sky *(2019), which stars Natalie Portman as an astronaut suffering from PTSD in the aftermath of a space mission; and created numerous TV series, including five seasons of* Fargo *(2014–24), the Marvel Comics–inspired show* Legion *(2017–19), and, most recently,* Alien: Earth *(2025), a prequel to the 1979 Ridley Scott film. When interviewers emphasize the sheer breadth of his output, Hawley responds by sharing his professional motto: "What else can I get away with?" It's exactly this boldness and sharp attunement to the world around him that have come to define Hawley's high-wire acts.*

For this issue, Hawley was interviewed by actor and musician Jason Schwartzman, who plays the impudent son of a powerful crime boss in Fargo*'s fourth season. Schwartzman's storied film and television career began when he landed his first role, at the age of seventeen, in Wes Anderson's* Rushmore *(1998), beginning a long-standing collaboration between the two. With the release of Luca Guadagnino's* Queer *and Francis Ford Coppola's* Megalopolis, *2024 was an especially triumphant year for Schwartzman, who had roles in both, as well as the lead in Nathan Silver's critically acclaimed film* Between the Temples, *in which Schwartzman plays a doubt-ridden cantor heartened by his friendship with his former elementary school music teacher. Contributing to his status as a veritable indie darling, Schwartzman once played drums and wrote songs in the successful alternative-rock band Phantom Planet, and later made music for his solo project, Coconut Records. Recently, in* New York *magazine, Schwartzman described some of his favorite things. The list includes magnets, laminators, fabric markers for covering up coffee stains, his wife's candles, and Boggle, about which he writes, "How did they create this game? How did they know what letters to put on what square? How did they do that? It is amazing. It's probably one of the most important things in my life."*

—The Editors

I. "IT'S WATER, WATER, WATER, SMALL TALK, SMALL TALK, AND THEN—CHARM THEM"

JASON SCHWARTZMAN: Let's just talk. So, you're here in LA for how long?

NOAH HAWLEY: Just until Friday. Although there's a screening of [Robert Eggers's] *Nosferatu* on Friday night. And I'm like, Do I stay? It's the kind of thing that's hard with the kids—to say, *I'm gonna stay another night to see a movie that I could see later*, but Eggers is gonna be there. I could do it, but when you're in our business, you're gone from home so much that it feels like it's gotta be really worth it to ask that of them.

JS: I know, I totally agree. There's a band called Fontaines D.C., a really great band from Ireland. I've been literally following them. I seem to always be missing them on tour wherever they're going. And so when I was in Manchester recently for work, it turned out they were going to be playing in this area not far away called Wolverhampton. I thought, OK, I have to do it. Even though I'll be wrapped, I've got to stay this one extra day. And then I just couldn't. I was like, What am I gonna do, go to this concert and not be with my kids?

NH: This business, in this town especially, will always ask things of you, and you've got to learn where your boundaries are. I've just learned to be like, *No, I'm good*. If it can be convenient for me, we'll do it. If not, it's fine. I don't need it.

JS: When you talk about not doing something and having your boundaries, I wonder if there are any types of things you wouldn't do, more out of nervousness or fear. Like, you've gotten numerous awards, and you've had to go into these rooms that are full of all these people. I'm so fearful in those kinds of public situations, or I used to be, at least. Are your boundaries only family and time? Or are there things that hold you back from things you're afraid of?

NH: No.

JS: Really?

NH: Long question, short answer.

JS: Exactly, yeah.

Natalie Portman as Lucy Cola in Lucy in the Sky. *Courtesy of Searchlight Pictures.*

NH: Yeah, pretty much. We grow up as nervous young men with social anxieties, but I had a moment early in my career when I realized there's a performance aspect to the job. I remember clearly one day thinking, Just go in and put yourself out there, even if you don't feel it. And it's easier the more I do it. A big part of this business is sales, right? A pitch is a very artificial thing. You walk into a room, make small talk, segue into the pitch. You do your pitch, and then maybe there will be a conversation about the pitch, and then you leave. It's water, water, water, small talk, small talk, and then—charm them. It's such a skill to be good at that, and you don't want to deprive yourself of it. I always say you've got to be good enough to get into the room, you've got to be good in the room, and you've got to deliver when you leave the room. If you can do those three things right, you've got a career.

I remember we were in Chicago doing *Fargo*, season four. We had dinner: you, me, and [my wife], Kyle. You asked, "How do you do all the things you do?" And Kyle said, "He has no creative doubt." I hadn't thought about it that way, but it's true. When I do something and I like it, I don't have any doubt about it.

I will say what I've taken to doing when I go to these awards events: I have an agenda. I think, OK, here are the three people I want to talk to at this thing. Then, once I've talked to them, I can leave. So it's not just some amorphous thing you're going to. It's like, I want to talk to this person, I want to talk to their boss and maybe schmooze with someone else, and then let's just get out of there. Because a lot of those things, you're like, I'm going, but what's the point? Why am I doing it?

JS: When you're talking about your agenda, are those people you want to talk to?

Behind-the-scenes shots and film stills from Lucy in the Sky. *Courtesy of Searchlight Pictures.*

NH: Yes, those are people I want to talk to. It's such a funny business. There are some parties that you go to just to be seen in the same room as certain people. So they go, *Oh, right, you earned your way into this room.* The goal is always, as an entrepreneur—which is what I am—to be able to do what I'm doing more: I want to make more TV, write another book. You've got to be a good businessperson. I'm not romantic about Hollywood; it's all just people. I've never been invited to the White House, but I imagine that would be something I'd have a few nerves about.

II. THE LOGIC POLICE

JS: I will say, as someone who was in your hands [with *Fargo*], it's so nice to have a director without creative doubts, because someone's gotta be that way. You need someone that has a mission and has a way to do it. That was the greatest thing for me about that whole experience—the inspiration I took from you. How do you have such clarity about this? It's beautiful. It's so clean.

NH: Yeah, and at the same time, because I'm very comfortable—I know what the story is and what the scene is—I'm open. We're doing this together, and I want to know: What are your instincts? What do you think you should be in this room? Because being open to the process is important, not feeling threatened by other people's ideas.

At the same time, I said to FX in the first year of *Fargo*, "You can't make a Coen brothers movie by committee." Ultimately, someone's gotta be the Coen brothers, and in that case, it was me—especially if you're trying to do something a little weird or specific.

JS: And that has not been done before.

NH: Yeah. There's really only one note you ever get [from the network], and that's clarity. They'll sacrifice everything for it—the joke, the emotion, the moment. You have to fight that clarity note.

JS: Because you feel like sometimes you're losing too much.

NH: It's so reductive. And it's not how people watch things. You get this logic-police thing: *What's the backstory? Where does he stand on whatever issue?* But then it's a terrible story. As long as people are not actively confused, if they feel like they're in good hands, they'll go, *I don't get it yet, but I'm sure I will when it's time.*

JS: That makes it fun, because it feels like you're watching something grow as opposed to just being told something.

NH: My favorite moment in production is walking on set for the first time and thinking, This could go horribly. Because then you're really risking something. It's not just, Yeah, it'll be mediocre. It's like, No, this could be an epic fail.

JS: I love that thinking too. I feel like it makes you accountable, because we're all necessary on that set. Everyone's important and has a skill. It makes you afraid of wasting people's time.

NH: You know the first time you're directing and you're standing on a set and two hundred people are staring at you like, *What's next, boss? Where's the camera going? What are we doing?* Your mind goes blank in that moment. Over time, you learn to be OK with that moment, and go, "Well, what should we do next?" Then if it's silent long enough, people start offering you stuff, and you're like, "No, no, no."

You remember Mitch [Dubin], the camera operator? He's shot every Spielberg movie since *The Lost World: Jurassic Park*, and that's how Spielberg works. He needs the fear. He needs to show up going, *I don't know how I'm gonna shoot the scene*, and then walk the set, and then be inspired. That's the line I try to walk: between having a plan and being inspired.

JS: When you were talking about not having any creative doubt, I was wondering about your books. How long does it take for you to know whether or not a book is something at all? How long do you work on it before you go, Maybe this isn't where I want to go?

NH: All creativity is an act of play. So my approach to writing is "Yes, and." It's like improv. When an idea hits me, I'm like, Oh, I like that, and then what? There are a lot of people who go, Well, that's good, but could I do better? I figure if the idea could be better, then along the way I'll go, Oh, you know what would be better... I don't linger. I just go.

It's the same thing on set: Here we are and we've got the script and the actors and the lights and the cameras, but I need to be open to what is in this moment so I can play with the material. That doesn't mean the material itself is playful or comedic or whatever. Sometimes it's a super dramatic scene. Writing screenplays, you're telling the story with the camera, and what the camera is doing needs to be in the script. If it's like, *You walk into the room. There's a gun on the table*, I know that, editorially, I've got to see the gun. I've got to see you seeing the gun. So why not write it in? "Coming into the room, lost in thought; angle on the table; there's a gun; close-up on Jason; he sees the gun; these are the thoughts that go through his head." Sometimes it gets really specific. But that way, when people read the script, they see the movie.

JS: I remember that, as I read your scripts, it was like watching a show, but on paper. It was so evocative.

NH: Whenever you're asking someone to interact with your story, it should feel like your story. It's why I do the hair-and-makeup tests I do. I don't know how anybody else does things, but at a certain point early on, I thought, We have to show the studio or the network what these people look like in clothes and makeup. But instead of just having them turn to the right and move on, I was like, Well, we've got sets we've built, we have all the actors, here's an opportunity to put them in spaces together. To go, This is a protagonist and an antagonist: What's that vibe?

JS: It's so rare to have that, by the way. It's the coolest thing in the world.

NH: And then the actors get an opportunity to wear the skin of the characters without any pressure; there's no lines.

I just come up with these little vignettes. Now it's kind of a joke because I'll bring in a techno dolly and cranes to my hair-and-makeup test. But then I cut this thing together to music, and I show it to the corporation, and they go, *I see what this is gonna be. I see what the tone of voice is.* You could watch the hair-and-makeup test of season two of *Fargo*, or season one of *Legion*. These things are all out there. We did this one for *Alien: Earth* and it was super cool to feel like in two days you'd made a mini movie.

JS: For *Alien: Earth*, were there any pretests that you shot before that? Or is that also the first time you're doing it?

NH: It's the first thing. It wakes the crew up. It gets them behind the wheel of the car they have to drive. Because a lot of times you're like, This operator's never worked with this focus puller. You get that opportunity to start to share a common language.

I did this pitch once: I drove over, we had the small talk, and then it was time. And I said, "I was thinking on the way over here about what the segue should be from small talk to the pitch. And I was thinking that maybe I should talk about how my house was broken into recently and they stole my guitars. And then I thought, No, no, no, maybe I should talk about how I was watching TV the other night, and *Stripes* came on. I thought, Oh, we need that. We don't have that Bill Murray antihero anymore." And I went through a couple of things of, like, what the segue should be. And then at a certain point, it became clear that this was the pitch. It was a crime story about a Bill Murray antihero. You know what I mean? But everyone in the room was like, *What's happening right now? We're not used to this meta thing.* So the tone of that was also the tone of the show. It's a playful and inventive show.

JS: So smart.

NH: I just get excited about all the creative problem-solving. I have to imagine that Wes [Anderson] is similar. I know he's got things sort of planned out, but it's all playful.

III. SECRET WEAPON

JS: One thing I really love about you is—this will sound so cheesy, but I could ask you, *Can you describe hot water to me?* And someone could explain it, but I feel like you would say, *Give me your hand.* And you'd just put it under hot water and say, *That's hot water.*

NH: Thank you.

JS: It's so precise. As we said earlier: long question, short answer; it's like that. It's nice for actors who sometimes don't know what they're talking about. You have this ability to speak their language. It's a weird language, and you do it very well.

NH: The script is the best worst blueprint. No matter how good the experience of reading the script is, it's not the experience of watching. It's like the script for *The Shining*. Quality script. Watching *The Shining*: nothing like reading the script. The music, you know, the omniscient camerawork… My secret weapon is that I know what it's going to sound like.

JS: I want to talk about that.

NH: I have a score for a show recorded before we film. I talked with [composer] Jeff Russo in advance, and when I was location-scouting for season one of *Fargo*, I had, like, ten pieces of music, including the main theme that he had written. So I was able to sit on that bus going through that landscape listening to that piece of music and going, I know what the show is.

JS: How do you even explain to him what you're trying to make, based on the script?

NH: We talked about it at the outline stage, very early. I said that the score for *Legion* should sound like [*The*] *Dark Side of the Moon*, which is about as close to the experience of mental illness, sonically, as you can get.

JS: You're so detailed. Do you get hung up on things? I would be like, OK, electronic music. And then I would need three weeks to research, and I wouldn't end up doing it, because I would be researching.

NH: To bring up *The Shining* again, on season five of *Fargo*, I just wanted that Moog sound, the mood of it. You can only

Salvatore Esposito as Gaetano Fadda, Jason Schwartzman as Josto Fadda, and Noah Hawley shooting Fargo *season four. Courtesy of Elizabeth Morris/FX.*

play one note at a time. That's how that old synth works. There was something about that. And that's the opening music.

JS: Did you use a real old Moog?

NH: Oh yeah, Jeff always has instruments made. He has this crazy thing for *Alien: Earth*, this giant steel triangle with strings on it and you can bow it and hit it with a mallet. He found a guy in Germany to make it. When I said [*The*] *Dark Side of the Moon* to him, he went out and he found the actual patch cord synth, the same model they used on the album.

JS: The Synthi. That's so cool. I see him because our kids go to the same school. It's fun to be able to know that someone is a musician from a distance, because I'm just thinking, He's dropping his kids off, but he's listening to something right now in his head. He's working on something.

I loved, by the way, that score. It was so beautiful. Because also it was really jarring. There were frequencies and tones that you really can get only with those instruments, that you can feel on a fucked-up, deep level, that are unsettling. Truly low.

NH: It gets in your bones. I had it in my head early on that for season five of *Fargo* I wanted a version of "Toxic," the Britney song. I had this Irish singer Lisa Hannigan do this version of it. I didn't know where I wanted to use it, but when I got to the moment of Jon Hamm walking, this long walk—that was in the script when I wrote it. I wanted the camera to be on him from the moment he leaves the car all the way till he reaches that building. The network

Jason Schwartzman and Noah Hawley behind the scenes of Fargo *season four. Courtesy of Elizabeth Morris/FX.*

kept saying, "It's really long," and I was like, "I know, but look what's happening on his face: the transformation, this humiliation, becoming the man who's gonna be violent and vengeful in that moment."

I worked on the music with Jeff and I would go, "It drops into a rhythm here: I don't want that. I want it to be more bare, more haunting and atmospheric."

JS: You're musicians.

NH: Jeff and I can have very specific conversations. It's helpful. And we also talk about where not to use music, which is often the most important thing.

IV. EMPHASIZING THE RIGHT SYLLABLE

JS: If all directors could talk about music like this, it'd be great.

NH: One of my biggest regrets is—this will kill you the way it killed me—we recorded the score for *Alien: Earth* at Abbey Road Studios in Studio One, and I was gonna go, and then I couldn't get away. It was the last three days before they did a remodel, so it was probably the last time that room was gonna sound exactly like it did when the Beatles recorded in there. So I got the chance to sing at Abbey Road, but I just wasn't there to do it.

JS: It would kill me. But I would accept it. You can't do anything about that.

NH: I have a lot of conversations with Kyle where she says, "Should I have done this?" And I just don't do that. What's the point? We did it that way, I'm happy with my life. There's rarely a thing where I go, *Oh, I should have made a different choice.* I have a pretty low resting heart rate.

JS: You do, I know.

NH: I have this line that I use when I'm hiring people: never hire anyone who climbs four flights of stairs to get to the second floor. Some people just work too hard. You're putting the emph-*a*-sis on the wrong syl-*la*-ble. The day is long, there's a lot to do. We know it's impossible, what we have to do every day, and somehow we manage to get it done most of the time.

We had this conversation. I don't know if you remember, because you were really nervous about a big scene. I said, "Well, picture your favorite scene in your favorite movie." You said the "I could have been a contender" scene. And I was like, "They filmed that on a Tuesday between four and eight o'clock, and I guarantee you, if they didn't get it right, they came back the next day." You've just got to show up and be in the moment. That's the job. What's crazy is there's so much money at stake. And the time constraints are ridiculous. But my job is to make it so that you have no idea. If we need to take more time, we'll take more time. But I'm also able to make choices on the go and economize. I'm a pragmatist on some level.

JS: How hard is it for you to do a show where you can't direct every episode? When you're getting footage back and you're watching it, is that a weird feeling?

NH: It's tough. I don't like watching other people's dailies, because when I see the director's cut, I don't want to know what they shot. I want to experience it in the story. I want to watch it like a viewer. Sometimes someone will call me and say, "I think you should see what they did yesterday," and I will take a look. But my career is full of moments of me in the editing room going, "Why did you do it like that?"

JS: But you figure it out.

NH: I called you in season five, and I was like, "I'm gonna

send you some lines and I need you to record them into your phone." And you must have been like, What is this? It was a tiger documentary.

JS: I loved it, though.

NH: That was because it was a scene didn't have that Coen brothers tone. Some of it was definitely my fault. The mother-in-law of Juno Temple's character has her committed to a mental hospital, and the guys show up to take her, and Juno was playing it real: anguished, desperate, trying to escape. And I was like, Oh no. If we do the real tone in this moment, we cannot be funny again in the whole episode. But budget-wise we were up against it. I couldn't afford to reshoot. They had shot this whole thing, and she's in the mental hospital and she's tied up. So I was sitting there and I just thought, We've referred to her as a "tiger" several times. What if we call the episode "The Tiger" and do this David Attenborough voice-over about the tiger? You know, *It may look like the tiger is giving up, but look closely. Even now, she plans her escape*. In that way, we salvaged the tone. But that wasn't in the script; that was me in the editing room going, Oh no, what am I gonna do?

V. "I DON'T LIKE AUDITIONING ACTORS. I WOULD RATHER GO, LET'S CALL JASON"

JS: Tell me about the new *Alien*. How do you even begin to switch into that kind of thing? I don't know anything about it, but the idea of you and that together is what's so exciting to me, your visual language and your language-language combined with this other kind of terror and presence.

NH: It's not a career I ever thought I would have, reinventing classic movies—but if I have a secret to it, it's that I really just try to figure out what the original made me feel and why, and then re-create those feelings by telling a different story. It started with *Fargo*. What's interesting is that in the first season of *Fargo*, my sole focus was on making a Coen brothers thing. With *Alien: Earth*, my sole focus is not on making something that feels like a Ridley Scott or a James Cameron movie. The original *Alien* is a class story on some level. It's blue-collar. It's almost like *Waiting for Godot* in space. It's all about not getting paid.

The thing that makes it interesting to me is the reveal that Ian Holm is a synthetic being. You thought this was a monster movie; now it's a whole other thing. You have the parasitic monsters of our animal past, and then this AI future, and they're both trying to kill humanity. I was like, Well, that's an interesting space to tell a story. That certainly feels relevant to our moment, sandwiched between bird flu and OpenAI.

JS: Is it hard to explain a vision to actors? One of your greatest skills as a leader is getting everyone to believe in the same thing, which is basically impossible to do. You're so good at it. You have everybody fighting for the same thing. How do you get people to fight for something they haven't even seen yet?

NH: I always love the moment, especially in *Fargo*, of showing the first hour to the actors for the first time. That show is a lot of moving pieces on a collision course, and it often starts off feeling like five different movies, and then by the middle they're all converging into one.

I rewatched the first couple of hours of our season recently. That whole opening twenty minutes, which is the history of true crime in Kansas City, with the different film stocks and the mug shots that we did, and those Blue Note album cover transitions. I went in with a lot of stylistic ideas that I think came together in a really interesting way. But how can you know until you see it? You're like, Oh, that's what we're making.

JS: I don't really take pleasure in watching anything I've done, but that was the most fun. To work with someone you like is sort of the equivalent of a band you like asking you to go on tour with them. You don't usually get to join the band. Unless you're like Johnny Marr, who joined every band, in a great way. But it's such a joy to love something and then to be part of it.

NH: I remember when we met, we had that lunch off the Paramount lot, and I was pitching you this season, and then halfway through the meal I realized you were pitching why you should be in it. I was like, I'm trying to get him to do it; he's trying to get me to hire him. So clearly we both want to do it.

JS: Oh my god. For me, that was the only time in my life when a dream really did come true. If you could have asked me, *What was one thing you would want...*

NH: Hearing that is meaningful too. Jennifer Jason Leigh wrote me a letter about *Fargo*.

JS: She's so incredible in that.

NH: That role calls for a certain withering disdain. I had been thinking a lot about the Brits, because those Maggie Smith types, they can do withering disdain like nobody's business. But I got that letter from Jennifer and I was like, Well, of course, Jennifer. There's something about the Americanness of it, too, that is a very different brand of disappointed mother.

Sydney Chandler, who is the lead in *Alien: Earth*—she flew up to Calgary while I was shooting season five, because she wanted the job. There were other actors who I Zoomed with and she was like, *No, I'm getting on a plane. I'm coming up there to get the job, to have dinner and talk.* That's meaningful to me. I try to tell my kids, "Make the effort, you know, show them that you want it." You've got to chase the thing you love. Because everyone's coming at you when you're casting things, and everyone's got ideas. I have my own ideas. I think, What about Andrew Bird as an undertaker? The network's like, "Well, is he gonna audition?" I'm like, "Oh god no, he would be terrible, that would be the worst audition you ever saw. But I think I can get the performance out of him." I don't like auditioning actors. I would rather go, *Let's call Jason.*

JS: You've probably been asked this a million times, but I don't know the answer. When is something for a book, and when is something for a movie, or are you only doing one? Is it very clear to you what something is?

NH: There's one idea I have that keeps shifting between mediums. But usually there's a couple of rules, if you think about how media exists in time. In television, we're basically interacting with the culture in real time. You're like ten to twelve months off. A film takes five to seven years to get into production. A book can take three to seven years to get into the world. So on some level, if you want to deal with a cultural moment that's of this moment, you want to do it in television. With a film, you don't know in five years what we're all going to be doing. Hopefully this film is gonna hit, and things do, but you had no idea when you started the process that it was gonna be a movie of the moment. A book is a similar thing.

JS: My last question is: If you write a book, obviously you're picturing something. If you're writing a script, you're picturing something.

NH: Yeah.

JS: But is it the same kind of picturing?

NH: No, it's different. It's still visual, but it's different. The amazing thing about fiction is that you can jump a hundred years in a sentence, and the audience, the readers, will stay with you. A book is so much more expansive than a script. A script is this finite, specific thing, because if I don't make it specific enough, you don't get it. I started as a fiction writer, but I think I'm a very visual fiction writer. I didn't read a lot of scripts before I started writing them. Nobody ever taught me how to do any of this. I was just like, Well, this seems like how you would do it. You would say what they see and then have the seeing be filmmaking. Otherwise, it feels esoteric.

JS: A director once told me that being a director is kind of like having sex. You don't know exactly how other people do it. You have your way of doing it, you think it's pretty good, but you're maybe kind of jealous. You don't really want to go visit someone else's set, unless you're into that.

NH: I rarely go to other people's sets, but I did go, when I was in New York, to [Jason] Bateman's set for his new show. I think Laura Linney was directing. I was there for an hour or so, and I was like, Yeah, this is obviously the filmmaking process. I see it. But it's not my film. But I think that's interesting.

JS: I think so too. ✯

LISA LUCAS

[PUBLISHER, EDITOR]

"I'M AFTER HUMAN EXPERIENCE, DEPTH, ENRICHMENT, AND LIVING MORE LIVES THAN I'M ALLOWED TO LIVE."

Books that taught Lisa Lucas how to love reading as child:
Bunnicula
The Pushcart War
The Baby-Sitters Club series
The Lonely Doll

The first time I met Lisa Lucas was around 2012, through mutual publishing friends, in the early days after my arrival in New York City. While I was a wide-eyed foreigner trying to cobble together a new life for myself in the States, and a not-yet-published writer working in publishing (the worst combination if you want to be a good writer), Lisa was a pistol. She was quick to give advice, quick to smile, always happy to chat for a few minutes, and always keen to connect with others. Even back then, I could sense that she sought people, not their status.

When I met Lisa, she was the publisher of the nonprofit magazine Guernica. *She went on to serve as the executive director of the National Book Foundation for four years, before accepting the position of senior vice president and publisher of Pantheon Books and Schocken Books, imprints of Penguin Random House. She was the first Black woman to hold each of these positions. The publishing industry as well as the media like to remind everyone of this, as if they were the ones doing the work that Lisa was doing all along.*

Illustration by Kristian Hammerstad

Lisa entered book publishing in a nontraditional way, taking a very different path from the more common publishing-career trajectory of starting as an assistant and then climbing the ranks over time. Before Guernica, *she had been the director of education at the Tribeca Film Institute, and before that, the telefund manager at Chicago's Steppenwolf Theatre. Back in the day, she interned at* Vibe *magazine. She approached each of these opportunities with boldness and bravery. In June 2020, when publishing executives faced strong pressure to bring diversity and equity to the table, Lisa tweeted: "Anyone need someone to run an equitable publishing house? *raises hand*." In July 2020, Penguin Random House hired her.*

In summer 2021, when my debut novel, The Nursery, *went out on submission, our relationship changed from that of mere acquaintances. She was the publisher who saw something in my book, and I was the author who wanted her to be my editor. Our first call about the book was as filled with giggles as it was with shrewd, constructive feedback. It's hard to describe how much it meant to hear someone say, "I want you to take your book as far as you can," when your story focuses on a subject (postpartum depression) that I felt few wanted to take seriously in literary fiction, but Lisa encouraged me to write without limits. (The book went on to become a* New York Times *Notable Book of 2023.)*

Within the traditional corporate publishing structure of Penguin Random House, Lisa competitively acquired book manuscripts for both Pantheon and Schocken, served as the editor of select titles, and started building a work family, which meant hiring and strengthening a new team. Even while she handled these large and demanding roles, she took a granular interest in the work—like fighting to get spot gloss on my cover, which mean that the words a novel *would shine as if dripped out of a blurry postpartum nipple. I wanted her to succeed so badly that for a while I didn't see that she was tasked with being responsible for a tremendous amount of work—perhaps an unreasonable amount of work for any one person to manage.*

Barely four years into the gig at Penguin Random House, Lisa was let go, and I, like many others, lost my publisher and editor. For anyone who might not know, it can take twelve to twenty-four months for a book to be published after it's been acquired. Sometimes longer. Still, even in this short amount of time, Lisa had relaunched the Australian writer Helen Garner in the US, published debut authors like Laura Warrell (whose novel Sweet, Soft, Plenty Rhythm *became a finalist for the PEN/Faulkner Award for Fiction and the Barnes & Noble Discover Prize), and championed award-winning British writers like Diana Evans, Sathnam Sanghera, and Guy Gunaratne on this side of the pond. In my eyes, she was just getting started—now we will simply have to see what she'll do next.*

—Szilvia Molnar

I. A HIGGLEDY-PIGGLEDY PATH

THE BELIEVER: Looking at everything that you've done throughout your career—and correct me if I'm wrong—I always saw you as a searcher. You and I got to know each other when you were working at *Guernica*—

LISA LUCAS: What was I like back then? Back in the *Guernica* days?

BLVR: I feel like you were this beautiful, forceful wind that swept in, wanting to connect and talk. You had a lot of passion and energy. You were always very warm and welcoming. But it also felt like you wanted a bigger challenge, both in the publishing world and beyond it. Do you recognize any of that?

LL: I've had this higgledy-piggledy path. I started in theater—I was raising money for a theater company—and because I got involved with the education department, I subsequently moved to a youth theater, where I worked on educational programs. Later, I went into film and I worked at [the] Tribeca [Film Festival], running educational programs there. Then I left and started at *Guernica*, which was this free online magazine. I went on to the National Book Awards, which was part of the National Book Foundation, an organization whose mission is making sure that literature is accessible to all. Then I went into commercial book publishing, which is one of the only industries that has the scale to move something to all Americans; it's one of the more reliable ways to disseminate information to a large block of American readers.

BLVR: Was your path connected to the type of upbringing you had?

LL: I was really privileged in the sense that I grew up in a family that was part of the arts. My father was a musician; my mother was an avid reader and cultural consumer. They were interested in plays and dance and theater and books—it made my life really rich, and it made their lives really rich. I always felt kind of confused when I was super young and I'd be in spaces and say, "Oh my god, this book is so good," and people would be like, "What?" They were not on the same page. It was never a question of being dumb or smart. It was never a question of being a snob or not. It was never a question of anything other than the fact that everybody is exposed to different things. For me, I saw that we were not offering invitations broadly to American society to participate in nuance. Every single thing I've ever done has been driven by this question: How do you make a thing accessible to more people? Whether it's raising money so that literacy programs can thrive, or marketing those programs, or publishing a book and trying to think about the best way to get it in front of a lot of people—for me that is the most exciting work; it's where my energy comes from. I'm a book person and a nerd, but I'm also an extrovert, someone who is very communicative and loves conversation, interchange, argument, and debate.

BLVR: Could you give me an example of what that might have looked like, in a tangible way, at the National Book Awards?

LL: Well, one random anecdote about my time at the NBA that's perhaps related: I was on a train and I remember meeting a couple and chatting with them about books and work and life and politics. At some point, I had gone on so long about the book I was reading that I just handed it to the wife and told her I had another copy at the office and a different book in my purse. A few months later I did an interview with CBS News and mentioned that the National Book Foundation [NBF] needed financial support to grow. A few days later, I got a check for five thousand dollars from the couple on the train.

BLVR: That requires a lot of openness on your part and also an interest in other people, which can be a rare thing these days—to have the strength to connect with others rather than shut down. It seems as though you also feed off that. Returning to your background, can you see where that came from?

LL: I don't come from cynical people. It's always been important to me to not be cynical. I also grew up with people who very much paved their own ways. They were like, *I'm not necessarily gonna do this the way that somebody else does it. I'm not necessarily gonna follow this rule or that rule, but I'm gonna actually chase the thing that makes sense to me.* For me, that made me feel like who I was and what I wanted to do was okay, that I didn't have to go be a lawyer or take on a more typical, well-understood professional career in order to be a person who had stability or success in this life.

One thing I like to share is that I'm much more exuberant than either of my parents. I think everybody was a little surprised when I came out with so much energy and personality. They always encouraged me to love what I loved without making me feel stupid about it. It's not about money. It's not about winning. It's about being open-hearted and working together to create a more robust and widely accessible cultural apparatus.

II. "I'M NOT AFTER MASTERY"

BLVR: You seem to read broadly and have so many different interests. I've always been jealous not only of your appreciation and knowledge of graphic novels, but also of your deep knowledge of nonfiction and international fiction.

LL: The life of a dilettante! The broad reading has always been with me. When we narrow our interests to these very specific lanes, sure, there can be mastery. But I'm not after mastery. I'm after human experience, depth, enrichment, and living more lives than I'm allowed to live. A lot of the books that I read as a young reader were recommendations from other people. And I feel like that experience of receiving good book recommendations and then actually reading the books made me an anti-snob.

BLVR: What are the specific books that have made a big impact on you?

LL: This is always such a difficult question. There are the books that teach you to love reading as a child: how I loved *Bunnicula*, *The Pushcart War*, the social nature of The Baby-Sitters Club books, the weird sadness of *The Lonely Doll*. And then there are the books that set you on a particular path in young adulthood—Zadie Smith's *White Teeth*, Paul Beatty's *The White Boy Shuffle*, Marguerite Duras's *Moderato Cantabile*, Robert A. Caro's *The Power Broker*, [Theodore]

Dreiser's *Sister Carrie*, [Edith] Wharton's *The House of Mirth*, [James] Baldwin's *The Fire Next Time*, the stories of Steven Millhauser, Mary Gaitskill, and Toni Cade Bambara. Each of these reading experiences was singular, and I consider them all dear old companions and return to them often.

You know, I do not need a book to carry me along. I'm happy to do the work with the book, to pick up what it's putting down. And I love that, but that's not the only kind of book. Books are tools. When I see somebody reading a self-help book, I'm glad they're reading a self-help book, regardless of whether I read self-help. Other people's preferences don't change my own taste. I just think that books are for everyone, and that means different kinds of books can exist. I think there's value in all of them—or most of them. They all mean something to someone.

BLVR: Over the years you've talked about the mentors you've had in your life. I get the impression they have been a driving force, a way for you to feel supported in your desires, goals, and visions. How have your mentors entered your life, and how have these relationships changed over the years?

LL: Some people teach you a lot and then leave your life, while others are there with you the whole time. For me, *mentor* is such a specific word. Loosely defined, the word—as I think you mean it—is really about anyone who takes an interest in you and teaches you something in the spirit of wanting to see you succeed. I've been so lucky. For every person who believes in you, there are three million that don't. It is vital to have the support of people who actually want to help you grow in a world that can be very difficult and challenging, especially for a young Black woman. I'm not super young anymore, but for a lot of my career I was considered precocious in the things I was doing. I think you need a lot of support when you're a woman, when you're young, when you're a person of color, when you're making big changes in an industry and thinking about how to challenge existing systems.

BLVR: What have you learned from your mentors? Do you feel comfortable sharing who they are?

LL: No one does anything all by themselves. You need people to hire you, train you, teach you, recommend you, correct you—in a caring and non-scary way, which is often the difference between a mentor and a boss—congratulate you, and keep you humble.

I've always had the same personality that I have now—enthusiastic, energetic, casual, transparent, opinionated, confident, determined, and, of course, a host of terrible flaws. And for this reason, especially early on, and extra-especially as a precocious young Black woman, I've always needed support. And I've been so lucky to find it. In particular, I could call out three people without whom I would not be me [in publishing], and those are legendary publisher Fiona McCrae, NBF board chair and Open Road [Integrated] Media CEO David Steinberger, and my age peer the brilliant Flatiron publisher Megan Lynch. They have been believers, guides, champions, gentle scolders, teachers, and forceful reminders to keep going when I want very badly to give up. I wish I'd had people like them in my life when I was in my twenties and early thirties. Ultimately, mentorship is about believing in the future and not being intimidated by the fact that life will go on when we retire and cycle out; and that until every American wants to call themselves a reader, the work continues; and that we are all working in lockstep, aside from the folks for whom this is solely about the money and prestige.

I don't know that my career would be possible without champions like them, because I've never felt that the world was straight up ready to receive me without somebody else cosigning me. It's challenging even now. I left book publishing, and the question is: Will I go back? *Can* I go back? At present, there's no indication that I can.

BLVR: This makes me think of how writers also need champions. As a writer, you can write for yourself, you can look for an audience, but at the same time you need those champions in your corner who speak out and say that what you're doing is good and interesting so you don't feel crazy or completely alone. None of us can do this alone, in any of the roles we have in publishing. At Pantheon, you introduced me to every person who was working behind the scenes to make my book come to life—from the assistant who sent galleys out to prizes, to the copy editor patiently going through my comments, to the cover designer who put together incredible mock-ups. It was very moving and made me feel much more connected to what we were trying to accomplish with the publication of *The Nursery*.

LL: I think it's so important to be collaborative. It's really important for there to be a family around anyone doing difficult work. A work family, if you will. Even if it's temporary or project-specific. But to create that kind of support and collaboration, to say, *We're all on the same page and this is what we're going to do*—I love that kind of work. It's one of the most beautiful things to watch a book be made, or to put on an awards show. It's a hundred thousand steps. I've never been an isolationist. When people think about books, they might think that the writer and the editor sit down and they work together and then there's a book. No! There are so many different people that are part of the process. Of course, the writer is the show. Without the writer, there's nothing. But the support that turns the writer's work into a book is such interesting magic.

I've worked pretty consecutively since I was fifteen. Part of the joy of working for me is being a part of a team. I don't know if my work will be as team-driven, moving forward, but I'm still imagining all the different ways I can be of service and work purposefully and successfully.

III. "THERE'S PLEASURE IN THE GROWING"

BLVR: You mentioned that you've been working so hard since you were fifteen.

LL: I don't know if it was "so hard," but yes, working.

BLVR: But even the fact that you've dared to try different art forms: I'm very impressed by that.

LL: I'm getting a little old to be brave.

BLVR: What was one of your early internships like—say, at *Vibe*? And how does it feel looking back on that time now?

LL: Reflecting on it now, I think it's wild that I started interning at fifteen. *Vibe* was an incredible experience—at the time it was still owned by Quincy Jones and there really wasn't anything else quite like it. I worked in the less-sexy advertising department for the publisher and the president's assistant. I certainly felt super young and very far out of my depth, but I was pleasantly surprised that they were absolutely willing to let me do real tasks, like the college interns were doing. Mostly, I just learned that I really, really liked to work and that I loved the energy and collaboration of offices. A very cool thing to be into at fifteen, I know.

BLVR: In light of all the experiences you've had, do you know some of the things you would like to try next?

LL: Listen, I'm on the cusp of forty-five years old. A forty-five-year-old middle-aged woman. It's like a movie trope: life falls apart and you rebuild. This is the most difficult time, the most difficult part of your life, to have to reimagine everything because the world is reimagining you. I'm not this young, energetic breath of wind anymore. I'm grown. I may have a youthful spirit. I may not yet have a lot of wrinkles, but I am my age. It's an interesting moment. I think it's different for men at forty-five; a lot of them seem to be coming into their power. I don't think that I'm *not*—I'm not ready to toss in the towel yet at all, by any stretch of the imagination—but I do think I'm deeply in the middle of considering what it means to have both the opportunity and the need to reimagine who I am. So much of who I am and what I put my life into has been my professional self. Everybody picks things. You look on TikTok and you see these moms who are like, *I have twenty-three children and I'm homesteading, and that's where I've devoted all my energy*, which is its own thing. Some people are careerists and spend their time working. Some people are family people. Where I've devoted my time, my space, my energy, my love, and my passion has been to my career, and it's not been for the sake of winning. If you had asked me when I was thirty what the next fifteen years would be like, I wasn't dreaming of any of this stuff. I was dreaming of getting things done.

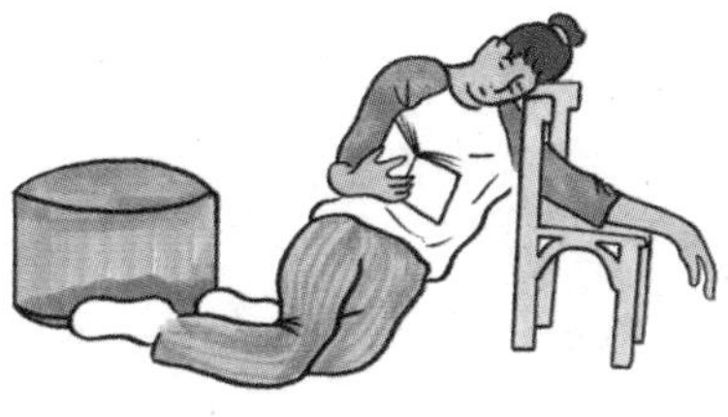

BLVR: I wanted to come around to the idea of work. As a non-American, I feel that Americans have an obsessive mind around work.

LL: A psychosis.

BLVR: Exactly, and that a person's value is connected so deeply to their career or achievements. How do you feel about all that? If your career has brought joy and knowledge to a lot of people, where in all that do you want to focus on yourself? What in all that brings you joy?

LL: There's this Faulkner quote. It's actually one of the epigraphs of Studs Terkel's *Working*, which is such an interesting exploration of what we do, how we do it, why we do it, and what it means. Faulkner says, "You can't eat for eight hours a day nor drink for eight hours a day nor make love for eight hours a day—all you can do for eight hours is work. Which is the reason why man makes himself and everybody else so miserable and unhappy." Work itself implies labor, difficulty, having to do something. But there's nothing else that we can do for all those hours. We want to be useful. I don't know what pleasure is outside of work, because usefulness and purpose are my joys. They are my whys. I don't know if I want to be stressed out and attached to my smartphone and computer and smartwatch three thousand hours a day for the rest of my life. But for me, my sense of purpose is work, and so my sense of joy is also tied to work.

Of course, it is beneficial to have some time to reflect and sleep and read deeply. That is one of the pleasures I've gotten back. Whether it was at the foundation or when I was working in book publishing or even in those *Guernica* years, the hustle was so extreme that I really lost the ability to just pick up a book I felt like reading—read it, enjoy it, and sink in. That is a reclaimed joy that I think this time is providing. I don't find a huge amount of joy in rebuilding unexpectedly, but I recognize the gloriousness of being able to look at a blank slate and say, Who am I and what will I be? There's pleasure in the growing and the being and the thinking and the learning, but I've also taken such great pleasure in my work. It's electric and addictive.

IV. "NOBODY WANTS TO FEEL LIKE A MASCOT"

BLVR: You've been a public figure throughout the years. Are there things you want people to know about you that you haven't gotten the chance to express?

LL: Look, publicity is so superficial, right? I think I became a "visible" person when I started at the National Book Foundation. That visibility happened because there hadn't ever been a person of color—let alone a woman of color—in charge of running that institution. It was 2016, and we were beginning to engage in a conversation about what equity and inclusion and diversity meant inside these different institutions. I wish people would think more about why my role was so overexposed and why there needed to be such disproportionate coverage of an arts administrator who can tell a good joke and likes a sequined dress—because that coverage tries to make it seem as though things have changed when they haven't. It's important to think about the pressure that that exposure puts on a person: we need to feel collectively like we're doing better, so we're going to put all this onto one human. Why not do the work to actually make things equitable rather than just highlight my one little corner, which is going to make my life harder to navigate, and my work harder to navigate?

I'm not shy. I neither hate nor crave attention. I feel neutral about it. I feel like a lot of the media and the publicity and the visibility has served my goals. Some of it is my own semi-compulsive need to communicate using Twitter and Instagram. But that also comes from being engaged deeply in conversation and connection, which is the ultimate root of my love of books and music and dance and theater and film and visual arts and the arts community. I'm really lucky that I have a point of view, and that I get to share that point of view, and everybody doesn't have that opportunity. That has been helpful, but it's also been an enormous pressure because of the focus on my identity. There's no universe in which events would have unfolded in this way without my identity being what it is. No one wants to feel used. Nobody wants to feel like a mascot.

Also, it'd be nice to go through difficult things privately, but that isn't always an option, for me at least. Of course, I could have just logged off my Twitter, but it's not a choice for my personality. I'm not a hider. My dad died. It was important to me to be open about my grief. Right now I think I'm in a moment of very public exploration. If everybody's gonna be wondering, *What is she gonna do?*, then I might as well have that conversation.

BLVR: And in all that, even if you're not shy, it doesn't mean that you don't need care, or support, or patience, or respect.

LL: Yeah, I'm human. There's the communication that happens on social media, which I find very comfortable and supportive, actually, like a blanket—I'm really invested in that community. But then there's the media, where you can end up regardless of whether or not you actively chose to participate in it. I find that more challenging. It's a lot of scrutiny.

But yeah, of course you need care. Every single one of us is just a person. Again, we're communicating with each other using the internet all the time, which then creates an abstraction: you no longer become Szilvia; you become an avatar—I can see your Instagram picture in my mind's eye right now, if I close my eyes. Even if there's connection, it can become dehumanizing. I think we have to really figure out how to change that. Every decade, every century, every generation, it's *How do we become human in these new contexts?* People can seem strong and be quite weak. People can seem weak and be quite strong. It's very obscure when we're all hiding behind the internet.

V. PREPARING FOR THE CYCLES

BLVR: Can you share a little bit about where you are in your life right now, mentally and work-wise?

LL: I'm taking a year off; I'm on this sort of accidental sabbatical. It feels like a good time to be rethinking the future. Right now, we're just past an election, and we have no idea what the years are going to look like. Everybody's in a state of panic in my universe. There's so much in the discourse about banning books, about whether or not people should stay on Twitter/X... I think of the freedoms that we've enjoyed throughout the entirety of my life and over the course of many, many generations. One really worries. So I think it's a good time to sit back and look at the landscape and ask, Where are readers? Where are publishers? Where are the arts? Where is the funding? What are the challenges? What can we do to create a safer future, a more expressive future, one where we have a multiplicity of voices that are well read and where events are well attended?

BLVR: Yes, perhaps I should mention that we are recording this right after the 2024 election, and our interview will be published in the spring. It's almost like we're talking into the future. How does that make you feel?

LL: It's really hard to be optimistic in times like these. We've been through a pandemic, a racial reckoning. We've been through a backlash to the racial reckoning. We've been through book bans, elections, uprisings, riots. Also, when you look at books, you have a completely changed marketplace. It looks nothing like it did eight years ago, sixteen years ago. It's in its most challenged spot ever in a lot of ways, specifically when you think about the literary world—I'm not talking about whether or not Colleen Hoover is selling books.

I was on the subway the other day, and I always count how many people are reading physical books. It was this incredible day when there were, like, twelve people reading. It felt like 2006. They all had their hardcover books out and one was reading Ta-Nehisi Coates's *The Message*. Somebody was reading a classic. Somebody was reading a work in translation. It felt like, OK, the work I do is actually present here in this space with these strangers. It was a reminder, for all the days when I sit on the subway and don't see people reading those books, that people are always still interacting and interfacing with books and art.

It's easy to get frustrated in these dips and these moments when things are not necessarily going the way you hoped they would go. Remember that it's all just cycles. The job for me at the moment is thinking about how to be ready for the next cycle, how to keep strengthening the audience and reminding people that despite the challenges within the book industry, books possess great value and bring great joy and are of great import. And that when we think about the politics we're living through, a book is going to be one of the things that can give you the most information, insight, and depth of knowledge. It's a good time to lean in.

A lot of people are confused about what's happening. I always say: If you want to think about the American conservative movement from the 1950s on, read Rick Perlstein. His books make what's happening now and how we arrived at this place more legible. For me that's a comfort. Comfort isn't just a sweet, fun book that makes you feel good and has a happy ending. Sometimes it's about knowing more and feeling more empowered. So I'm optimistic. Things are getting more confusing and more complicated, which is not great—we're all going to need more information. And we also need relief. What happens to my nervous system when I read a book for an hour is that I become one with that book, and for that hour I'm not engaging with all the issues and problems outside in the world. That, too, is a real gift. ★

SISYPHUS IN THE CAPITAL

CRIME, PUNISHMENT, AND THE LEGACY OF TRINIDAD AND TOBAGO'S FAILED COUP

by Eskor David Johnson

Two of them leaped the wall into the backyard where my friends were having a hang: bandits with pistols already drawn so that no one would do anything courageous. Even on the CCTV footage, through which I and everyone else would later see the unfolding, time seemed somehow warped to the surreal pace of small tragedies, where ultimately no one is harmed, no one killed, but the lingering weight of such possibilities makes even the clocks struggle to move. Both the assailants wore bandannas around the lower half of their faces, like highwaymen. My friends relinquished their cell phones and jewelry. Then the bandits had them keep a distance and scaled the wall again with an ease and fluidity that was not absent of grace, and were in and out in what had arguably been three minutes, but which for all of us watching—for those boys I knew from school now forever preserved in the soundless archives of victims—was certainly far longer. I haven't made a habit of stopping by that backyard in the time since.

> At 6 p.m. this afternoon, the government of Trinidad and Tobago was overthrown. The prime minister and members of the cabinet are under arrest. We are asking everybody to remain… calm. The revolutionary forces are commanded to control the streets. There shall be no looting.

These were among the remarks delivered to the people of Trinidad and Tobago on Friday, July 27, 1990, by Yasin Abu Bakr, né Lennox Phillip, a former police officer turned community organizer, whose paramilitary organization, the Jamaat al-Muslimeen, had, just a half hour prior, overseen the capture and command of the islands' lone TV station, as well as Parliament, where the prime minister and members of his cabinet were being held hostage. *Community organizer* here being a loose term. The Muslimeen's attempt at a coup covered a six-day span, during which the police headquarters was bombed, a member of Parliament was killed, intense looting spread throughout the capital anyway, and Prime Minister Arthur Robinson, when ordered by his captors to instruct the mobilizing armed forces to stand down, using the megaphone provided, famously yelled: "Attack with full force!"—an act of heroism for which he was shot in the leg. While under duress, Robinson was also coerced into signing an amnesty agreement granting the usurpers full clemency in the eyes of the law, should anything go wrong with their plan, a scheme so harebrained and legally dubious that it is only with a sense of incredulity that we can imagine him to have signed his name to the agreement, believing that anything can be promised to men who are soon doomed to die.

Illustration by Andrea Settimo

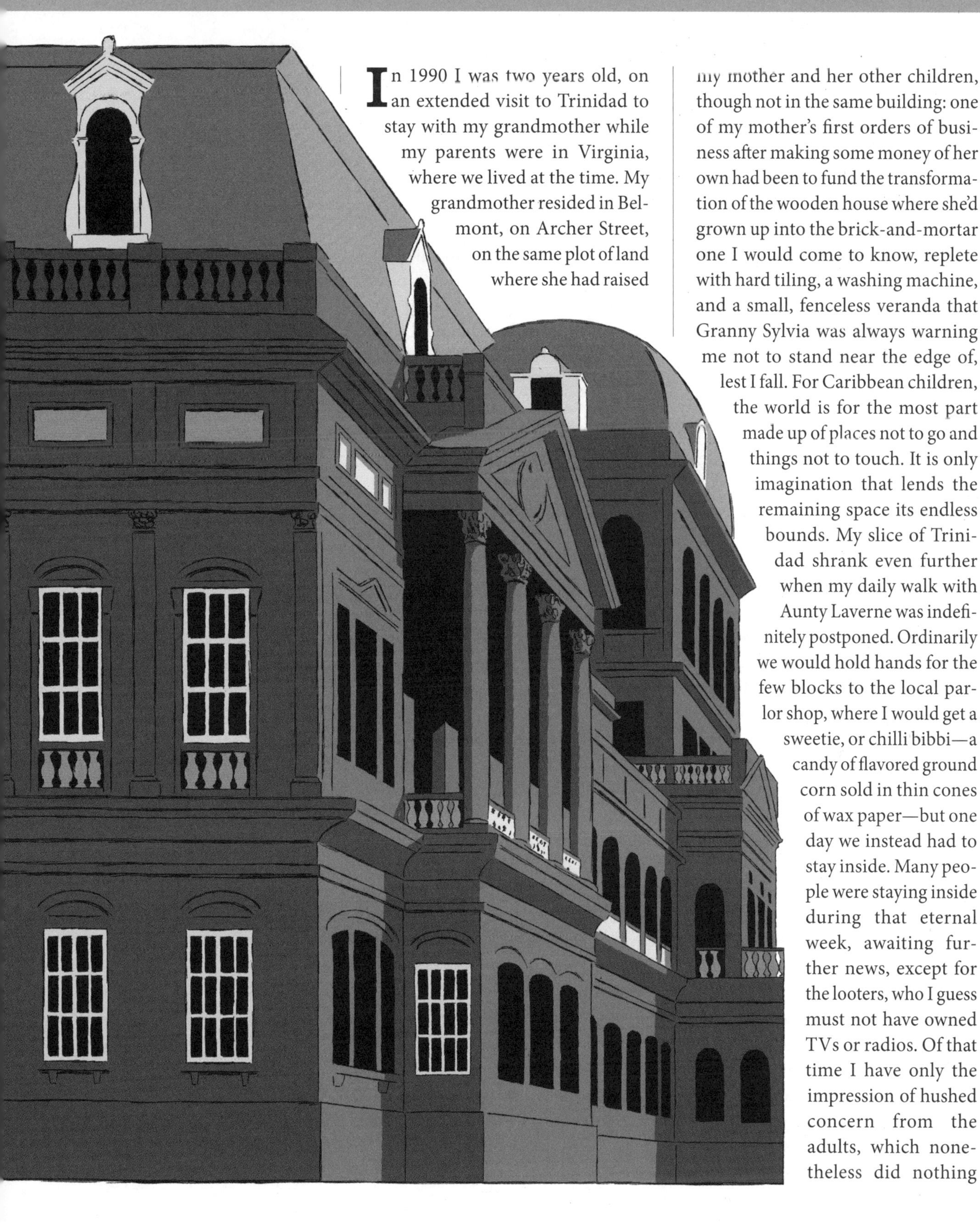

In 1990 I was two years old, on an extended visit to Trinidad to stay with my grandmother while my parents were in Virginia, where we lived at the time. My grandmother resided in Belmont, on Archer Street, on the same plot of land where she had raised my mother and her other children, though not in the same building: one of my mother's first orders of business after making some money of her own had been to fund the transformation of the wooden house where she'd grown up into the brick-and-mortar one I would come to know, replete with hard tiling, a washing machine, and a small, fenceless veranda that Granny Sylvia was always warning me not to stand near the edge of, lest I fall. For Caribbean children, the world is for the most part made up of places not to go and things not to touch. It is only imagination that lends the remaining space its endless bounds. My slice of Trinidad shrank even further when my daily walk with Aunty Laverne was indefinitely postponed. Ordinarily we would hold hands for the few blocks to the local parlor shop, where I would get a sweetie, or chilli bibbi—a candy of flavored ground corn sold in thin cones of wax paper—but one day we instead had to stay inside. Many people were staying inside during that eternal week, awaiting further news, except for the looters, who I guess must not have owned TVs or radios. Of that time I have only the impression of hushed concern from the adults, which nonetheless did nothing to dampen the general excitement that characterized my vacation as a whole. I was reportedly so happy during the six months I spent in Trinidad that when, one day much later, a pair of strangers entered our home and told me I had to come with them, I refused and hid behind my grandmother's leg. They were my parents, back from the US to collect me, and whose existence I had in the meantime forgotten. Only my dad's promise of a bicycle was enough to lure me away; he was sitting on the edge of the washing machine and miming a pedaling motion in the air. "Bicycle! Look, bicycle." I agreed to go with the strangers. In my early understanding of material gain as a substitute for love, I had taken a vital step toward becoming a Trinidadian.

As a matter of fact, the amnesty agreement did stand up in the courts, and in the months following the surrender, arrest, and jailing of Abu Bakr and his forces, the cynical validity of their legal loophole would soon become apparent. In a ruling from Justice Clevert Brooks, based on the precedent of governments acting in the interest of restoring national stability, the forcibly signed amnesty agreement was considered part of a negotiated settlement aimed at ending the coup and was thus valid and binding. Which is to say: they were free to go.

Absent of wars, not every nation is afforded so obvious a fork in the road between who they are and who they might have been. One such moment in Trinidad's recent history was the failed attempt in the late 1950s to form, alongside nine other islands, a West Indies Federation. With the federation's shared currency, open borders, and collective government, we might have grown resilient against the meddling influences that were the World Banks and IMFs of the time, whose entrapments of debt we have been long in recovering from. The other moment was this coup, which offered us an alternative destiny, not in its potential success (this seems too unlikely), but in the response to its failure. In setting the men free, we exposed ourselves to a mocking revelation, one that is the unspoken fear of any new nation that was once a colony: that we were an unserious country. Our laws were written on paper and nowhere else; they had not made their way into the mettle of who we were. As a Nigerian friend of my father's once opined upon hearing the story of the Muslimeen, "Say what you want about Africans. At least we have the good sense to round up our traitors for the firing squad."

By thirteen I was attending my first house parties in Trinidad. My family had finally moved back full time about two years after my initial visit, and the four of us—including my younger sister—lived in Maraval, a quick ten minutes from Belmont and Granny Sylvia, who had suffered a minor stroke in 1994. My sister and I attended the same elementary school until we each sat the national secondary school entrance exam three years apart and matriculated to our respective single-sex institutions.

The house parties would gain traction as rumors, shared from boy to boy, weeks in advance. There was to be a big bashment in Diego Martin, for example, promising pretty girls, lots of dancing, and a chance to wear your cool

FICTIONAL NEWSPAPERS IN LITERATURE

- ★ *The Weekly Volcano* and *The Spread Eagle* in *Little Women* by Louisa May Alcott
- ★ *The Daily Beast* in *Scoop* by Evelyn Waugh
- ★ *The Current* in *New Grub Street* by George Gissing
- ★ *The Daily Punctilio* in *A Series of Unfortunate Events* by Lemony Snicket
- ★ *New York Rowdy Journal* in *Martin Chuzzlewit* by Charles Dickens
- ★ *The Daily Prophet* and *The Quibbler* in *Harry Potter* by J. K. Rowling
- ★ *The City Light* in *The Bonfire of the Vanities* by Tom Wolfe
- ★ *The Trinidad Sentinel* in *A House for Mr. Biswas* by V. S. Naipaul
- ★ *The Daily Post* in *Sharp Objects* by Gillian Flynn
- ★ *La Vie Française* in *Bel-Ami* by Guy de Maupassant
- ★ *The Eatanswill Gazette* and *The Eatanswill Independent* in *The Pickwick Papers* by Charles Dickens
- ★ *The Gammy Bird* in *The Shipping News* by Annie Proulx
- ★ *The Daily Bugle*, *The Daily Planet*, and *The Gotham Gazette* in Marvel Comics

—list compiled by Lula Konner

clothes. I would go, only after much cajoling from my parents, mostly to end up in a flock with my friends, not knowing what to do next. In these new evenings of adolescence there lingered something fraught and ecstatic in that darkening terrain, as if, left to our own devices, we had stepped beyond the eyes of society into a jungle of our own making.

Then soon enough I stopped going to any house parties at all, not for not knowing where they were, but for there no longer being as many for anyone to go to. People were nervous. It was 2003. There was a story of a bandit leaping the wall of a house party in Moka and robbing everyone upstairs. There was an old, recurrent story of a young boy at a birthday party drowning under mysterious circumstances, which, though unsolved and never tied to any bandits, did nothing to assuage the pervading sense of there being dangerous strangers everywhere. Kidnappings were so persistent that they earned a dedicated segment on the evening news. One of the older boys at school, a cricket star from a wealthy family, was kidnapped for several days and held for ransom. My friend's father was kidnapped, with the kidnappers' intent, no doubt, of holding him for several days for ransom, but managed to escape from the back seat of the car and flee into the bush. A girl walking to a bus stop, I had heard, was kidnapped for several days and held for ransom but instead killed. There were rumors that the army was involved. There were rumors that narcotraficantes were involved. There were rumors that one of the oligarchic Syrian families—who had suffered the common indignity of having one of their own kidnapped for several days and held for ransom—had flown in a European hit man to deal with the perpetrators, and that was why no more Syrians were being kidnapped: it was just everybody else. No one was really sure.

One place you could be sure was in your house, behind locked doors. Dusk was the time to find out exactly where your loved ones were, and to go from one place to the other only with precautions, like those mice who seem to gather themselves before darting along the edges of rooms so as not to be noticed. Crime made children of us all, shrinking the world until it is comprised mostly of places not to go and things not to touch, times by which to tuck yourself into bed until the bullies said so.

"Attack with full force!" Prime Minister Robinson had said on the first day of the siege, but the armed forces delayed, and it was not until several days later that Abu Bakr and his men were instead allowed to peacefully surrender and were escorted from Parliament. He would live a long life, Abu Bakr, maintaining his compound near the heart of the capital and occasionally suing the government, passing away of old age in 2021. I once met a retired solider who still regretted, with a measure of bitterness, the fact that they had not been allowed to go into the building with guns blazing and nip in the bud the bloody destiny we were instead set upon. Once a government is revealed as feckless, he argued, naked the entire time we thought they were wearing clothes, everyone feels they can do anything, criminals most of all. In the years since 1990, the annual murder toll in Trinidad and Tobago has ballooned to around forty people per one hundred thousand: enough to earn it a recurrent spot in the world's top ten.

Perhaps this is disingenuous. In fact, the annual murder toll had already been rising before then, and might ultimately have had more to do with Trinidad's increasing role as a drug-shipment route between South and North America. It was this worsening situation, as well as the lack of economic opportunity for an underserved Afro-Trinidadian population, that Abu Bakr had wanted to stand against. Conditions in Trinidad and Tobago were ripe for a social explosion. The price of oil, our major export, had suffered a drastic decrease in the 1980s. A newly elected government had promised major reform in 1986, but instead had dallied and delayed.

Yet in taking matters into his own hands, Abu Bakr joined a long, ancient list of reckless men—and they have all been men—for whom the state is seen as a matter of opinion, and who always arrive at the same divine insight that the best way of fixing it is to run it themselves. The exact day that Abu Bakr's insurrection began marked the last on Earth for Gideon Orkar, a Nigerian soldier who some months earlier had seized control of a major radio station and called for the removal of five states from the Nigerian federal union. He was overpowered, imprisoned, and executed by firing squad at around the same time that Abu Bakr was addressing the people of Trinidad and Tobago. Later that year, down in Argentina, army colonel Mohamed Alí Seineldín led his second unsuccessful uprising, a kerfuffle that managed to rack up a death toll of fourteen within a scant twenty-four hours, then sputtered away from general lack of military support and led to his eventual imprisonment. In August 1982 there was air force officer Hezekiah Ochuka, president of Kenya for six hours, who captured a major radio station, explained that the economy was "in shambles due to corruption and mismanagement," and who in his haste to overthrow the government somehow overlooked recruiting the army to support his cause, and so was overpowered, caught after fleeing to Tanzania, extradited, and executed by hanging a few years later.

So many things can go wrong when attempting to overthrow a government that it boggles the mind that any have ever been overthrown. Whether the conspirators are somewhat bumbling, such as the rebels in Laos in 1973 who had both the airport and the radio station they had seized recaptured by government forces in just a few hours, or tactically excellent, like those in Venezuela in 1992 whose highly orchestrated plan was thwarted, in part, by inclement weather, the challenges they face, always within narrow windows of opportunity, are more likely to triumph before their new regime does. These heirs of Sisyphus are scattered across nations, the futility of their tasks matched in degree only by the seeming inevitability that another one of them, somewhere in time, will try again.

The problem, of course, is that some governments should be overthrown. Except that the matter of deciding which ones those are too often falls upon these juvenile tacticians, nearly comical in their blunders, devoid of equanimity, who even in their occasional successes promise mostly a rearrangement of the previous administration's faulty parts instead of a replacement. Their sole strategic advantage is usually the general sense of disbelief with which a populace tends to react to such an affront to the system. Always, before the appropriate forces can spring into action, there is that interminable standstill, made longer by the audacity of violence, when the minutes are warped, and all seem to be wondering, Is this really happening?

For Americans on January 6, 2021, such confusion was further compounded by a substitution of the cast that rendered the events unrecognizable to many: an insurrection taking place not in some distant brown country with sweating exotics, but in pristine Washington, DC, mostly by "real Americans" holding smartphones, who had booked hotels on their credit cards weeks in advance. Still, in keeping with the theme, they marched upon the Capitol, armed, high on outsize notions of corruption, injustice, and the need for a new order. Arguments that President Donald Trump—at whose behest they were there—did not attempt an actual coup tend to center around how impromptu the happenings felt. But they never have a plan, these people, or the plans are so foolish as to barely qualify, consisting primarily of the two-step process: (1) take over a major building; and (2) I am in charge. They rely on their own failure to prevent them from finding out who they would become beyond that limiting horizon.

So, too, did Americans, then, have their chance to grapple with the question of who they really were, and whether their ideals could withstand the transition from abstract concept into practical application. (Although, to be fair, grappling with "who they really

---

PHILOSOPHIES PRACTICED OR EMBODIED BY FICTIONAL ANIMALS

- ★ Taoism, Pooh, *Winnie-the-Pooh*
- ★ Marxism, the entire barnyard, *Animal Farm*
- ★ Epicureanism, Baloo, *The Jungle Book*
- ★ Hedonism, Toad, *Frog and Toad*
- ★ Pragmatism, Mrs. Fox, *Fantastic Mr. Fox*
- ★ Cartesianism, Tock, *The Phantom Tollbooth*
- ★ Absurdism, the Cheshire Cat, *Alice's Adventures in Wonderland*
- ★ Stoicism, the Caterpillar, *Alice's Adventures in Wonderland*
- ★ Machiavellianism, Puss in Boots, *The Fairy Tales of Charles Perrault*
- ★ Empiricism, the Cat in the Hat, *The Cat in the Hat*
- ★ Virtue ethics, Aslan, *The Chronicles of Narnia*

—list compiled by Maya Segal

are" is a preferred American pastime.) The nearly four years' worth of prosecutions levied against Trump ranged in scope and scale from the long shot to the surefire, a federal indictment for attempting to use fake electors, or state RICO charges aimed at bringing down his entire organization of coconspirators. In the end they culminated in nothing more than a graveyard of botched cases, the most ambitious of which was derailed by a romantic relationship between two Georgia prosecutors, one of whom showed the other such preferential treatment as purchasing tickets for a Caribbean cruise. Over this period, the sense of pervading unreality—that an act so brazen, so televised, and so, yes, harebrained could go so unpunished—was for one half of the country quasi-religious proof of illuminated destiny, and for the other an indicator of a world they hadn't realized was beyond their understanding: in these matters of political surrealism, they had not had as much practice as we of the third world. Most irreverent of all was Trump's eventual return to the legitimate process of electoral politics and his victory in last November's election, thereby reclaiming the power with which he could subsequently pardon his fifteen hundred or so coconspirators—a convenience of circumstance that even Bakr himself would surely have envied. As if, in having tried to break into a house by way of a crowbar and smashed windows, Trump instead had resorted to walking to the front door and ringing the doorbell, then had the residents let him and his bandits inside before the police could arrive.

Abu Bakr gave frequent interviews in the following years, never hesitant to express his ongoing displeasure with Trinidad and Tobago's state of affairs, and to continue to press his case for how much better things would have been under his command. Perhaps his talking points sound familiar: the collapse of law and order, a corrupt nation, the need for someone strong to step in. "Because I was in charge," he once offered by way of explanation for the lower crime rate in the years preceding his attempted takeover. "Before 1990, I was in charge of the ground, and when I came out of prison I left it." Whence cometh these cynical prophets, who help to make a mess, then point to it as the reason they should be in control of cleaning it up?

A national psyche is loosened when someone is allowed to publicly flaunt the agreements we have all made with one another. The damage from this loosening does not have to come now, but it does come. My Trinidad is a small one, made of familiar streets, people I already know. It is less that we live in fear than that we live with a sort of mortal resignation, one that stifles the ideas of what is possible long before they reach the potential stages of exploration and play that are the necessary precursors of growth. We understand that any stranger can be the last one you ever meet; that if the police are called, they will arrive late and may want to know why you are bothering them.

Rare is the failed insurrectionist who grows old walking about in the free air. Something satisfied and mocking settles into their gaze as a result, a glint of the successful heist that can never be extinguished. *Who are you as a people?* this glint says. *What kind of a country can you be that would let me get away with this?* ✯

MICROINTERVIEW WITH DUSTIN PAYSEUR, PART IV

THE BELIEVER: I've heard you talk about how, sonically, shoegaze music tends to be easily replicated. What are the more affective qualities of the genre that you try to tap into to avoid a generic approach?

DUSTIN PAYSEUR: I think there are so many ways to take it. If you take all the reverb, delay, and distortion off it, playing it unplugged, singing in a room with just a guitar, what do those songs sound like? They're like incandescent bulbs. They're warm and amber and purple, really dreamy and romantic. No genre sounds more like what emotions feel like—which is usually multiple things at once. I think shoegaze a lot of times feels both heartbroken and in love. Happy and sad. It's not afraid to be multiple emotions, where so many genres are just trying to be one thing. With shoegaze you're like, How does this song sound like making out and crying at the same time? [*Laughing*] ✯

PRETTY BAD POEMS *for* MOSTLY WORSE MOVIES

FREAKS (1932) SESTINA

DIRECTED BY TOD BROWNING

BUDGET: $310,000; BOX OFFICE: $289,000

We didn't lie to you, folks
Step right up to all conglomeration of oddity
The living torso, Johnny Eck the half-man,
The Siamese twins, save your disgust
For the vain trapeze artist and the censors
Gooble-Gobble, we accept you, one of us

Last night I had a dream about us
We lived in a tent among the carny folks
We weren't afraid before the censors
You had no arms, and I was an oddity
With no legs, and it was the oblivion of disgust
Together we were total woman, complete man

The villain of this picture is the strongman
The studio butchered it to protect us
Test audiences fainted from disgust
On set the cast was segregated from normal folks
No bearded lady or pinhead the real oddity
But how immoral moral outrage is in the censors

With *Dracula*, Tod Browning passed the censors
Because a monster is still a man
But in daring to suggest the dwarf is like us
Love becomes the fairway oddity
Hate comes naturally to natural folks
They regard radical equality with disgust

You dirty rats fill me with disgust.
We are serious weirdos, you're not safe behind censors
My family of complicated lovers is coming for you simple folks
For laughing and pointing because no man
Holds the spoon between our toes like us
But I don't miss what I am missing, commodity is the oddity

From behind the curtain, unveil the sensational oddity
From the vengeance of clowns, you recoil in disgust
From under the muddied wagon wheels, fear us
Trim the minutes, but humanity is beyond the censors
All I have is a mouth, says the snake-man,
And there is a knife in it for the upright arrogance of folks

The conjoined twins are no oddity to the more-than-mortal man
Love will not become disgust, here we are all goodly folks
Except the censors. Gooble-Gobble, we accept you, one of us

INTOLERANCE (1916) PANTOUM

DIRECTED BY D. W. GRIFFITH

BUDGET: $2.5 MILLION; BOX OFFICE: $1.75 MILLION

In the hanging gardens, your butthole they kisseth
Why make one movie when you can invent the anthology?
You can do what you want if you're D. W. Griffith
And spend thousands on elephants all out of chronology

Why make one movie when you can invent the anthology?
Movies should move so behold this gross spectacle
And spend thousands on elephants all out of chronology
The silent-screen Christ is low-key heretical

Movies should move so behold this gross spectacle
Thematically, a spinster is a lot like a Huguenot
The silent-screen Christ is low-key heretical
Throw banquets and idols of Marduk into the Cuisinart

Thematically, a spinster is a lot like a Huguenot
See how suffragettes cause a strike to fuel their demonstration
Throw banquets and idols of Marduk into the Cuisinart
These liberal freaks will pay for dissing *The Birth of a Nation*

See how suffragettes cause a strike to fuel their demonstration
You can do what you want if you're D. W. Griffith
These liberal freaks will pay for dissing *The Birth of a Nation*
In the hanging gardens, your butthole they kisseth

THE ADVENTURES OF PLUTO NASH (2002) DIRGE

DIRECTED BY RON UNDERWOOD

BUDGET: $100 MILLION; BOX OFFICE: $7.1 MILLION

Dear Mother, I regret I shall never return from the moon
There is no atmosphere or joy, my jibes at best jejune
This is no more a comedy than Pluto is a planetoid
And I am always forgetting to plug in my pet android
Adrift in excess, kindness is but a prop
To think that I used to be *Beverly Hills Cop*

Better that my infamous face never comes across the vidphone
My friends have fled, I am in debt and second to my clone
My empty life is barren craters, the plot is full of holes
We were fools to think we could get away with bribing Harry Knowles
Such a lavish production, if there were but a little mirth
This makes *Blade Runner* look just like *Battlefield Earth*

MEGALOPOLIS (2024) ODE

DIRECTED BY FRANCIS FORD COPPOLA

BUDGET: $120 MILLION; BOX OFFICE: $7.6 MILLION

Thou father of gods and rumbler of fish
Thou wine-drunk auteur of an Ayn Rand folly
Self-financier of utopia as glorified screen saver
A filigreed fart in the face of cinephiles
What imperium doth dictate such helmet-hair'd boredom
By wit of Romans or club kids or what-the-fuck-ever
To conjure gasps of relief for Shia LaBeouf?
But what doth it mean? Dideth Dustin Hoffman just perish offscreen?
What ponderous inflection? Why a subplot devoted to Jon Voight's erection?
Don't let the now destroy the forever. Do it yourself.

CUTTHROAT ISLAND (1995)

OULIPIAN CONSTRAINT (NO GRATUITOUS PIRATE PUNS)

DIRECTED BY RENNY HARLIN

BUDGET: $115 MILLION; BOX OFFICE: $18.5 MILLION

Ahoy off the port bow, I spy a tax haven
I'll cast my wife, Geena Davis, while our rings are fresh-graven
To buckle swashes with Modine, though his come-ons are pervy,
Avast ye, my swabs, your hides riven with *advanced vitamin C deficiency*

I'll bankrupt the studio for a honeymoon gift
She'll do her own stunts to conceal our fond grift
Shoot cannons, sink sets, to expense I am numb
Yo ho ho and a bottle of *tastefully spiced Bacardi black label overproof*

Say "Aar," pet a monkey, feed Polly a cracker
I'll hire a historical consultant, but later I'll sack her
If critics climb aboard and tell me it stank,
I'll hold them at sword-point, they'll all *face civil judgment from an ad hoc civil jury*

Oh no, the IRS, somehow they found me
To save the rating, I cut the blood down profoundly
Raise the skull flag and hide our doubloons in the sails
If anyone talks, I'll say that *the deceased seldom report their experience to the living*

The budget we blew, but it's worse than my fear
Geena Davis divorced me for killing her career
Now I'm stuck making prequels, and Geena, they mock her
My marital dreams sunk to *the aquatic storage closet of one Davy Jones*

SPEED 2 (1997) VILLANELLE

DIRECTED BY JAN DE BONT

BUDGET: $160 MILLION; BOX OFFICE: $48 MILLION

Do not speed gentle into that cruising of control,
A bus can be a boat if the summer so demands
Rage, rage against Keanu not reprising his role

A sequel alone will dig us out of this hole
So we will hitch our Jet Ski to the bro from *The Lost Boys*
Do not speed gentle into that cruising of control

Willem Dafoe is on the loose, revenge is his goal
"If I had my health, why am I acting all crazy?"
Rage, rage against Keanu not reprising his role

Sandra Bullock's eyes forsake the road for her bankroll
Dog-paddling for some nice chick flick on the shoreline.
Do not speed gentle into that cruising of control

Extras smelling a free vacation flock to the punch bowl
If UB40 be the Muzak of reggae, then flügel on
Rage, rage against Keanu not reprising his role

Our fair vessel won't stop as it plows full slow
This block won't bust itself, so charge the Caribbean
Do not speed gentle into that cruising of control,
Rage, rage against Keanu not reprising his role

SPEED RACER (2008) SONNET

DIRECTED BY LANA AND LILLY WACHOWSKI

BUDGET: $120 MILLION; BOX OFFICE: $43.9 MILLION

Speed Racer is his name and his game is the same
Neck and neck with motorists of all nationality
With cuts galore and colors to crowd out the frame
And gadgets to narrowly dodge vehicular fatality
Red pill, blue pill, this time choose Dramamine
Greenscreen sets grate, CGI irks, the rest just annoys
Like stochastic chases to shame Steve McQueen
I guess it's never too early to license the toys
Even engines are lightweight with a script this clunky
Your minds are so blown you better go hatless
Some problems can't be solved by casting a monkey
If you think this is indulgent, wait for *Cloud Atlas*
Yet if you don't go for broke, you're just driving stick
Sugar highs so high that you can't feel your dick

NOTHING BUT TROUBLE (1991) ACROSTIC

DIRECTED BY JAN DE BONT

BUDGET: $165 MILLION; BOX OFFICE: $48 MILLION

Two hot entrepreneurs never oughta sought entertainment
Lest outrageous ooky killers suspect lust is kerfuffling everything
Apposite Dan Iykroyd, Chevy Khase

CATS (2019) BALLAD

DIRECTED BY TOM HOOPER

BUDGET: $210 MILLION (WITH MARKETING); BOX OFFICE: $75.5 MILLION

Ian McKellen is a befuddlesome fellow
A thespian knighted by the Queen
But he's not afraid to play feline
Though the effects are obscene
A revue so off-Broadway it wound up in hell
A valley so uncanny, it slopes into ravine

Lo, Persnickertybush and Frumfelictysnatch
For all I know, these cats are theoretical
Cockroaches dance, something about memory
For no reason at all, they keep saying *Jellicle*
Did the gummies kick in, or am I literally dead
The tacked-on faces from post are barely
symmetrical

Sing muse of Elba and Swift and Dame Judi Dench
A cat is a cat, not some kind of mutt
To the Heaviside Layer these house pets aspire
Belting out show tunes with the cockiest strut
The West End's hairball is hipster's delight
Release the butthole cut

MOONFALL (2022) HAIKU

DIRECTED BY ROLAND EMMERICH

BUDGET: $146 MILLION; BOX OFFICE: $19 MILLION

The moon is no good
Smug for a rank satellite
Stay the fuck up there

BABE: PIG IN THE CITY (1998) PASTORAL

DIRECTED BY GEORGE MILLER

BUDGET: $90 MILLION; BOX OFFICE: $18.3 MILLION

I wandered lonely as adorable pork
And bet the farm on urbane sophistication
Trading picket fences for a matte painting of New York
I daresay that these mammals spoiled my vacation
Sewers burble, scrapers keep the sky from view
No land for man, but for a pig, that'll do

DUNE (1984) SENRYU

DIRECTED BY DAVID LYNCH

BUDGET: $45 MILLION; BOX OFFICE: $30.9 MILLION

Oh, like stoned Prince Hal
The sleeper must awaken
Spice is no excuse

SUPER MARIO BROS. (1993) LIMERICK

DIRECTED BY ROCKY MORTON AND ANNABEL JANKEL

BUDGET: $48 MILLION; BOX OFFICE: $20.9 MILLION

There were once two plumbers of fame,
Freely adapted from a video game
They faced the King of Koop
But when the fan hit the poop
Their system did not entertain

The legend that John Keats died of a bad review is all-around uncouth; for one thing, critics seldom wield such power. Career suicide is a different matter. Oscar-nominated director Martin Brest has been persona non grata in Hollywood since the fiasco of 2003's *Gigli*, and the production of 2002's *Rollerball* was such a debacle, it landed its director, John McTiernan, in federal prison. From the cruel reception of visionary bombs like *The Adventures of Baron Munchausen* (1988) and *The Hudsucker Proxy* (1994) to the disastrous, industry-altering misfires of *Freaks* (1932) and *Heaven's Gate* (1980), these are tragedies about which bards sing and the ancients composed lofty epics. As Tim Robey writes in *Box Office Poison: Hollywood's Story in a Century of Flops*, "Failure fascinates… for all the reasons that surefire success is a drag." Ahead of their time or doomed from the start, each *Catwoman* (2004) or *Waterworld* (1995)—the latter actually exempt, as it made its budget back in international and video sales—looms eternal while Oscar darlings come and go. But as streaming makes mediocrity a sure bet, and studios are liable to delete anything risky enough to induce embarrassment, such artifacts of audacity will soon be a thing of the past. Below, in moribund verses ranging from pantoums to odes, I seek to honor pictures that spent a season in development hell. Let unpalatable lyrics illuminate unpopular entertainment. Having made my debut as a poet, I am happy to announce my retirement; Rimbaud had the right idea, and Dan Aykroyd got the message.

—*J. W. McCormack*

OBJECT

JOEY LAWRENCE'S FLANNEL

by Sam Shelstad

FEATURES:

- ✭ Ties around the waist
- ✭ Popular with girls
- ✭ Doubles as a superhero cape for your genitals

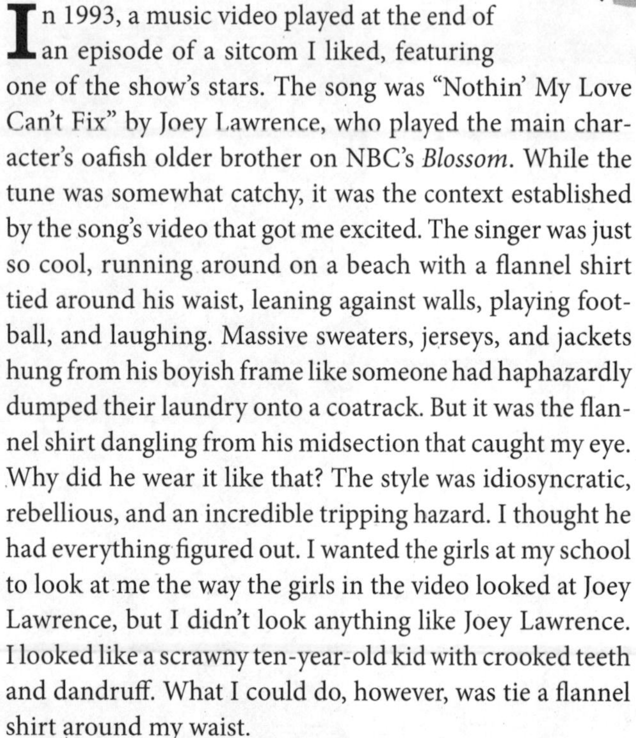

In 1993, a music video played at the end of an episode of a sitcom I liked, featuring one of the show's stars. The song was "Nothin' My Love Can't Fix" by Joey Lawrence, who played the main character's oafish older brother on NBC's *Blossom*. While the tune was somewhat catchy, it was the context established by the song's video that got me excited. The singer was just so cool, running around on a beach with a flannel shirt tied around his waist, leaning against walls, playing football, and laughing. Massive sweaters, jerseys, and jackets hung from his boyish frame like someone had haphazardly dumped their laundry onto a coatrack. But it was the flannel shirt dangling from his midsection that caught my eye. Why did he wear it like that? The style was idiosyncratic, rebellious, and an incredible tripping hazard. I thought he had everything figured out. I wanted the girls at my school to look at me the way the girls in the video looked at Joey Lawrence, but I didn't look anything like Joey Lawrence. I looked like a scrawny ten-year-old kid with crooked teeth and dandruff. What I could do, however, was tie a flannel shirt around my waist.

My small group of friends at school had taken notice as well, and thus we had our uniform. We borrowed our oversize flannel shirts from older siblings who worshipped Kurt Cobain, and tied them around our midriffs like superhero capes for our genitals. I had recently developed a crush on a girl in my class, after noticing the soles of her LA Gear sneakers light up at a school dance. I don't know if it was the flannel or the new confidence that wearing the flannel gave me, but after learning of my infatuation, the girl with the light-up shoes asked me to be her boyfriend. I accepted, and we immediately began avoiding each other until, at some point, she was "dating" another boy in my class. To this day, I have a recurring anxiety dream in which I suddenly remember the foggy existence of a strange girlfriend I haven't spoken to or even thought of in months.

The shirts were helping usher us into the first stages of puberty. One kid in our clique, Korey, began telling us stories at recess. Sex stories. We'd gather around him in our flannels, by the trees at the back of the schoolyard, and he would enthrall us with his latest titillating creation. In an incredible display of groupthink, and as a testament to the importance of sex education in schools, we all ended up tacitly deciding on a couple of things: First, when Korey reached the climax of one of his stories, all the boys gathered around him would simultaneously and instantly get erections. Or, at least in my case, pretend to. And second, it was somehow agreed upon that erections were incredibly painful and distressing. So when Korey reached his big finale, we would all grab our crotches and fall to the ground, yelling, "Korey, stop it! Korey!" I still remember one of his stories. It was a short one. Korey said, "You walk into your bedroom and there's a naked woman lying in your bed. And she's gorgeous. She says, 'Come to bed, baby.' You ask her what time it is. She looks at you and says, 'Sex o'clock.'" As soon as he said the words "Sex o'clock" we all collapsed onto the ground, holding our privates and writhing in pain, saying, "Aw, Korey! Korey, stop it!"

Joey Lawrence's foray into pop music is now an obscure piece of trivia that only a scattering of aging millennials half remember, but its sartorial impact on one rural Ontario schoolyard in 1993 was massive. Culturally and sexually, this music video became our *Ed Sullivan Show* Beatles appearance, our Eras Tour. "Nothin' My Love Can't Fix" is not looked on as a particularly good or memorable song now, but the music was never the point for us. It was the flannel shirts, fastened about our waists like the matching kilts that Highlanders wore into battle. Together, arm in arm—or hands on crotches, as we cried out in feigned distress—we marched toward adulthood. ✭

Illustration by Kyle Hilton

DELROY LINDO

[ACTOR]

"THAT QUESTION, 'WHO AM I?,' OR, MORE ACUTELY, 'WHO THE HELL AM I?,' IS THE BASIS OF EVERYTHING."

Historical figures Delroy Lindo has portrayed on-screen:
Baseball player Satchel Paige
Explorer Matthew Henson
US marshal Bass Reeves

I am racing the rain in the back of a London cab with Mr. Delroy Lindo. I was advised by a well-traveled friend to trust only this as a means of conveyance—the pug-nosed solidity of the classic black taxi, the encyclopedic patter of drivers versed in every alleyway and heath. We jounce over cobblestones, heading out of St. Pancras station toward the Young Vic theater on the South Bank. Mr. Lindo has agreed to answer what questions he can in the little time we have.

Outside, umbrellas amble along Brompton, Harrods breaks like a great ship over gray horizon—an anglophile's wet dream—yet I am transported by the actor's unmistakable brow and regal jaw to the smoke and storm of Oakland: Delroy Lindo in a velour black-and-white tracksuit as Aaliyah's overprotective kingpin daddy, Isaak O'Day, in the raucous Jet Li vehicle Romeo Must Die *(2000); Lindo rolling through the Gowanus projects, dispensing wisdom and ass-whuppings, as Rodney Little in Spike Lee's near-operatic crime drama* Clockers *(1995); Lindo in cowboy hat and black duster, cutting almost too* foine *a figure as legendary lawman Bass Reeves*

Illustration by Kristian Hammerstad

in Jeymes Samuel's beautifully defiant Black Western, The Harder They Fall *(2021).*

*My referents for this moment are deeply Black and American. B-boys and barristers aspire to the slow burn of Southern diphthongs tugging on the coattails of Adrian Boseman's Chi-Town courtroom manner (*The Good Fight *TV series, 2017–22). Bed-Stuy divas and Philly schoolteachers cream and sugar over at the Brooklyn drawl of Woody Carmichael beseeching a weary wife for more time, more space (*Crooklyn, *1994). Delroy Lindo embodies the inextricable intermarriage of urbanized Southern origins: an easy gait quick to turn from pirouette to dagger, an unflinching gaze that sifts softly into listening yet is honed sharp enough to mark the fool. He is Black America's quintessential older brother, uncle, deeply present and wayward father, enforcer, pusher, lover, with a voice modulated to the rise and fall of stride piano. Even as he "took an' tole us" who he was, channeling the swag and patois of West Indian Archie in Spike Lee's 1992 masterpiece* Malcolm X, *we continued to believe he was solely our own, and nothing could keep us from it.*

In his yet-to-be-titled memoir, slated to be published in 2026 by Little, Brown and Company, Delroy Lindo does not challenge the lineage Black Hollywood and ardent fans have assigned him, but instead asks that we see him—see him truly—as a child of the Diaspora, the son of a Jamaican émigré, a young woman who journeyed alone across the waters to London during the historic Windrush migration. Alongside some surprisingly personal and painful revelations, this history and his mother's struggles—to survive the inclement social and economic weather of 1950s London while raising a Black boy on her own so far from home—haunt the pages of a book crafted with the same lyricism and command the Tony Award–nominated actor is known for bringing to the stage.

I am here as part of a trio of early readers of his memoir—what Delroy calls the Triumvirate—that includes British writer and cultural critic Miranda Pyne and San Francisco–based author Diana Cohn. Delroy and I have spent much of our time visiting the sites of his childhood, including foster and group homes across southeast London, deep in the belly of white working-class British kindliness and aggression. Our cab ride was preceded by a day of riding shotgun in a black Peugeot, Mr. Lindo at the wheel, double-clutching, gearshift in hand, navigating narrow streets, talking about many things: art, longing, excellence and fear, the uncanny necessity of both exile and return.

—Erica Vital-Lazare

I. "A HUMAN POINT OF VIEW"

THE BELIEVER: I want to know how you get to a place where you are so real, in front of a camera, in front of an audience, onstage.

DELROY LINDO: It may sound glib, but it's practice, practice, practice. Thank god I took the time to train as an actor and to form a relationship with craft, so that when I'm working, no matter in what medium, I am attempting to pay attention to the technical aspects of the thing.

BLVR: I want to ask you about a scene.

DL: OK.

BLVR: It's a scene in *Get Shorty*. You're Bo Catlett, a gangster who is very obviously a student of film. He's dabbling in screenwriting and falls into something of an impromptu development meeting with John Travolta's character, Chili Palmer, a gangster breaking into movie production. You, as Bo Catlett, are in your element. You can feel your character thinking, Hey, I have someone here I'm talking to about the thing I love—moviemaking rather than gangstering. You're so beautifully ebullient. You want to share ideas about the script that Chili's strong-arming into production. Where someone else might have played the part with some sort of bluster or bravado, you instead become so vulnerable. There's an undercurrent of joy, but you don't know if you can claim the joy, because you're also a gangster in a confrontation with a gangster.

DL: Listen. Here's the thing. And this is where I believe technique comes in. For me, being inside the life of a character—and this, I think, speaks to the choices one could have made compared to the choice one actually makes—that scene is about two aspirational human beings trying to get a job done. And it's aspirational because we both want to be in the movie business. And here's a piece of material, a script, that will allow us both to transform. And in that moment, in that scene, he figuratively slaps me in the face.

BLVR: He shuts you down when you offer notes on his script.

DL: He shuts me down. But from a technique or technical

point of view, one does not go into that scene thinking, Man, I'm a gangster trying to do this other thing [moviemaking]. I go into it thinking, from a human point of view, I'm Bo Catlett and here's an opportunity to achieve a dream of mine.

Early on, I knew I wanted to pursue a certain versatility. I knew I wanted to create a range of different characters, which was the reason why, after I left the American Conservatory Theater in San Francisco, where I studied for two years, I went to New York, as opposed to Los Angeles: because I hoped that in going to New York and working in the theater, I would be challenged to do a range of different parts, and that's exactly what happened.

II. PLAYING THE FATHER

DL: I'm going to give you another example of deciding to see the humanity in characters whose actions are villainous: I did a film called *Clockers*, the third film I did with Spike [Lee].

BLVR: Yes, where you played Rodney Little, a Brooklyn drug lord.

DL: Rodney Little. I was doing a workshop at the University of Michigan, and many people asked about the scene in the car when I put a gun in Strike's mouth[1] [Strike is a drug dealer who works under Rodney Little]. I forget the exact question from the workshop, but it was something along the lines of *How did you do it? That scene?* And what I found myself saying was that the scene has nothing to do with the gun, per se. The gun is only the means. That scene is fundamentally about a parent scolding his child. "How dare you speak to me like that? Have you lost your mind? Who are you talking to?" *That* is something that any parent on the planet can relate to, and the behavior—the picking up of the gun—is just an outgrowth of that.

BLVR: Wow. You are talking about Rodney Little scolding his child—a situation that demonstrates love—with a gun.

DL: No question. It's been many years since I revisited it, but if you remember, there's another moment between Rodney and Strike: We're sitting in a car, and we're looking at a crack addict, a woman who was once a beauty and is now a shadow of herself. I remember this was in 1995, the height of the crack epidemic. I don't remember the exact words, but I say something to Strike like *I don't ever want to hear about you using this shit, you understand.* And that's not a threat. It comes out of concern.

There's another scene, earlier in the film, where we're watching a former mentor of mine, Errol, who is just disintegrating in front of my eyes, and it hurts. Having seen that, I turn to Strike and I ask him, *You eating, man?* And he says, *Nah, I ain't eating,* and I ask, *Come on, man, why you don't eat?* That comes out of love. There's a genuine caring the drug lord harbors for this young kid.

BLVR: You're also trying to save him but doing so with techniques born of your character's specific pathology.

DL: No question. But I think you know this: It's not my job to judge what's "pathological." It's my job to key into, on a human level, what makes [*snaps fingers*] Rodney tick. What kind of human being is Rodney, and how does Rodney do what he does?

There was a scene that was cut out of the film, but it was really important to me. The film is based on a book by Richard Price, and in the book, Rodney helps the kids with their homework. He's attempting to school these kids who are out on the block clocking, selling drugs—to educate them about how they should be in the world. "Y'all done your homework? Come get those books, man." It's complex. That's Rodney's MO, that's his humanity. And so while it's my job to key into those aspects of this human being, it's absolutely the audience's prerogative to look at me and say, *That dude is pathological.* But that has nothing to do with what I'm trying to build in that character.

BLVR: And that's the complexity—it goes back to what you were saying about being committed to exploring and expressing the full range of a character. He can be someone who loves like a father, but also someone who's willing to kill.

DL: Well, well. Before you said that, I was gonna say, *Loves*

---

1. The scene has become a cult classic: Mekhi Phifer, as Strike, is an hour late for his shift bagging crack. Delroy, as Rodney Little, pulls up, as a frustrated father would, and orders Strike to get his ass into the car. As they ride, Strike talks back. Little stops the car, thumps Strike in his notoriously sore gut, then grabs the nape of the young man's neck, forcing his head down, and places a gun in his mouth.

like a father, scolds like a father, disciplines like a father, in the particular ways that I [as Rodney Little] do those things. That's as far as I take it. Again, it's the audience's prerogative to label my activity, to describe my activity in the way they choose to. Does that make sense?

BLVR: It does. [*Laughing*] It does.

DL: Look, there's a wonderful thing with that particular character. As I said, it's based on a book, which I read twice before we started filming. When Spike told me he could introduce me to Richard Price, I said, "Of course I want to meet him." When I met Richard Price, he then introduced me to the human being that Rodney Little was based on. And one of the things I observed in this very charming man was that he liked to have a good time; he was a very funny man who just happened to do this other thing, to operate as a drug dealer. And in fact he insisted, "I don't do that anymore, man." Of course, it was an open question whether he still did or not. Again, not my job to judge.

BLVR: So you want to embrace the fullness of a character's humanity first.

DL: Yes. That's the actor's job. That's any actor's job.

BLVR: That takes me back to that moment we talked about in *Get Shorty*, where Travolta's character shuts you down. And it breaks my heart, the moment when your character says, "You don't know me."

DL: "You only think you do." Yeah. Now, if Spike had directed that film, I feel like in that moment right there I would have had more latitude to experiment. But it was a big Hollywood production with, like, bona fide Hollywood movie stars in it, and I was just coming off three films with Spike. If I had to do it again, I would play that scene a little differently. The thing is, you're gonna ask me, *Well, how?* I'm not sure what I would do differently.

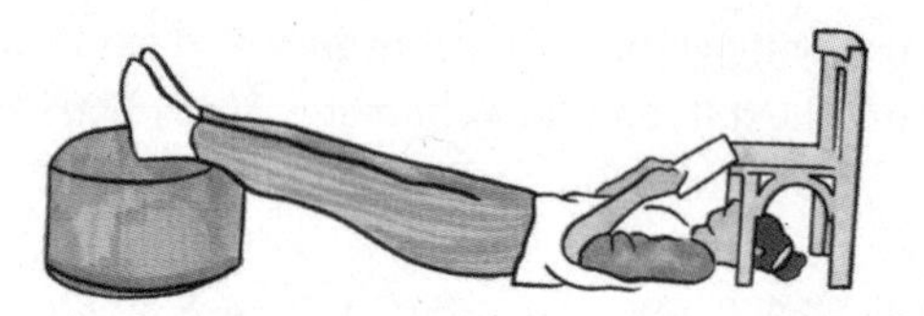

BLVR: OK, I *am* going to ask you: How would you do it differently?

DL: It would be more benign. I remember that I kind of scowl in that scene. I would show less of that.

III. THE WANDERER AND THE GUIDE

BLVR: Right now we're sitting in the Young Vic, in London, and I want you to tell me, please, a little bit about yourself in this space, your relation to this space.

DL: In 2010, I played Bynum in the brilliant August Wilson play *Joe Turner's Come and Gone.*[2] It was a creative return of sorts for me, because I had played Herald Loomis in the same play on Broadway twenty-two years earlier, in 1988. The interesting thing for me about playing Bynum Walker is that he is the nemesis—I'm saying "nemesis" in quotes—of Herald Loomis. I can chart my progression as an actor through those parts. There is the actor that I was prior to playing Walter Lee [in Lorraine Hansberry's *A Raisin in the Sun*] and Herald Loomis, and then there's the much improved actor, with a firmer grasp of technique and of myself as a creative worker, as a creative instrument. I had played Herald Loomis in 1988, and in 2010 at the Young Vic I came back to play Bynum Walker—two sides of the coin. It was a seminal experience for me as an actor to see the transformation from before 1988 to after.

BLVR: So you play the wanderer, and then you play the one who realizes that what is broken cannot be fixed by wandering.

DL: Listen, it's interesting that you say "the wanderer." To take that metaphor further—if in 1988 I was playing the wanderer, in 2010 I was playing the guide.

BLVR: Oh, damn.

DL: The brilliant thing about being the guide is that I'm

2. This is the second of Wilson's ten-play Century Cycle, chronicling Black life shortly after Reconstruction and into Jim Crow.

guiding without letting him know I'm guiding. I'm giving him these clues throughout the play, all of which Herald is rejecting. "You don't know me. You don't know me. Get up off me. You don't know me." And the secret is Bynum Walker knows Herald Loomis better than he knows himself. I love the play. I have a very, very strong connection to the work. So it was wonderful to come back here and play the part.

BLVR: Really, that entire process of coming back here to play the guide versus the wanderer—it mirrors your journey, personally and professionally. You said that you could see the transformation from before 1988 to after. It's a transformation of craft, but it's also a transformation of identity as someone who's coming into mastery. It's a continuous journey.

DL: All of the above. That question, "Who am I?," or, more acutely, "Who the hell am I?," is the basis of everything. And if the answer to that question is "I don't know," that's OK, because in actuality, we're changing from moment to moment, second to second. Synapses are those electrical charges inside ourselves—neurons that fire off in response to stimuli. And maybe the synapses are firing off that much more intensely when one is in the process of making work, of creating. Because in those moments when you're in pursuit of something, you have a heightened level of consciousness.

IV. "ON SOME LEVEL WE'RE EVERYTHING AND EVERYWHERE"

BLVR: So we've just come from an exhibit at the British Library, *Beyond the Bassline: 500 Years of Black British Music.*[3]

DL: Now, I don't know about you, but my synapses were firing off big time.

BLVR: Yes, very much so.

DL: Who we are on the planet, what our contributions have been, how our contributions have been undervalued—even an exhibit like that, with so many levels, only scratches the surface. Yet it's still formidable. When we were all rocking to the music, we're reacting and responding—the synapses were just firing off, man.

On some level we're everything and everywhere. For somebody like myself, an artist, the challenge is to embrace that knowledge and then to have that become part of my awareness about myself, about my history, about my mom... to give the animating force of our history its existence, to let it manifest in everything I do. How I raise my child, how I communicate with my loved ones, everything, all of it. Does that make sense?

BLVR: It makes absolute sense. I'm gonna take it somewhere because of your use of the word *we*. You mean all of us, right? All of humanity? All of who we are?

DL: Yes, well, I'm speaking about humanity, but I'm also speaking about African descendant humanity, because (a), to state the obvious, that's a particular reality, and (b) it's our reality.

BLVR: One of the video installations in that exhibit charts Black presence in Great Britain through the slave trade, then through migration—going back to the 1700s—and how music, or the sound of us, had to follow. There's a moment in a video from the 1960s when a young dub artist reflects on the class and race divide of the time, and the irony of Black music in white record shops, living rooms, and on the airwaves. He says, "Our music goes where we can't."

DL: I didn't see that, but I'm hearing you. That's profound, that's right.

BLVR: I think that speaks to all Black performance.

DL: Absolutely, because there are always those who are trying to constrain, restrain, suppress.

One of the reactions I was having fairly consistently at that exhibition was that I found myself responding to references to *the first Black artist to blah, blah, blah...* And I was irritated. And I think what irritated me was that the larger, dominant cultural and social forces allowed this one Black person in, so now they can say, *This was the first Black person; this was the*

3. Curated by Dr. Aleema Gray and MyKaell Riley, *Beyond the Bassline* is a multimedia exploration of the uncanny creation of Black music in Western spaces in the wake of the transatlantic slave trade, from classical to rhythm and blues, lovers' rock, hip-hop, and beyond.

first time. But don't you know there was so much more where that came from? If y'all would just... [*Laughing*] But they can't, they can't help themselves. Bless their hearts. So, anyhow. That is an acknowledgment of the power we come with, and one of the identifying, ever-present characteristics of Black people everywhere, but certainly of Black British, which is the attempt to bust out of the constraints. To take the chains off.

V. "MY SALVATION IS WITHIN MYSELF"

BLVR: You were on a promotional tour, I believe not long ago, for *UnPrisoned*, and you and Kerry Washington made an appearance on *The Breakfast Club*. First of all, I was struck by the ease between the two of you, the camaraderie, the respect, the appreciation. All that is apparent, particularly during a moment when Kerry Washington says of you, "Delroy is one of our national treasures." Do you remember her saying that?

DL: I do.

BLVR: And she went on to say you are part of her Mount Rushmore of great actors. Those are two references that fix you in a place and fix you in an identity. There's something in your cadence, in your aesthetics, and in your ethos that is deeply urban, urbane, Southern, all those things that I equate with a Black American identity. So that's what I mean by I'm "fixing you in place" in that way. But there's a complexity to that. I want to know how you feel about how I'm claiming you. I think a lot of Black American audiences do, and I want to know your thoughts about it.

DL: That's a beautiful thing. I can't say too much in response, because you said it. And what I mean by that is: Oh god, the kind of terminology you used, and the terminology that Kerry, as a colleague of mine, was using to describe me and to describe what I mean to her, how she's responded to my work, how she's responding to the two of us making work together—those comments, they speak for themselves. So I should allow them to speak on their own terms, and just live and breathe and be out in the world. My job is to continue to be a creative worker and make my best efforts at creative output wherever, however, I'm able. It's all fundamentally really affirming, because you're speaking about how you reacted and responded to my work as an actor. Right?

BLVR: Right. We've been talking about your ability to embody so many identities, which makes me think of DuBois's "double consciousness": two warring souls in one dark body. And you've got this dual—or I'll call it global—citizenship that's both Black and British. But in claiming you—as a stubborn Southerner and as a longtime film aficionado, particularly of Black film—I've always and will probably continue see you as a Black American actor. Even though you're a Black British actor.

DL: And that's OK. You know why it's OK? I say that my career was birthed in the United States. And you know why it's extra fine to say that, why it's important to say that? It's very simple, Erica. I could not have had the career or the life that I've had here. I could not.

BLVR: Why?

DL: Oh my god, how much time do we have? Because of empire, the continued entrenchedness of empire and how empire directly impacts and influences the position of Black people within the United Kingdom. There is a consistent, ubiquitous glass ceiling through which the majority of Black British actors do not go. They don't pierce that veil. What do they do? They go to America. Idris Elba. David Oyelowo. There are others. So I am completely fine being referred to as an African American actor. That's where my career was born, has grown, and has flourished.

BLVR: But we have so firmly claimed you in the pantheon of Black actors that I think I'm worried there's a part of us that refuses to see a part of you.

DL: I don't think so. I'm not quite sure why you're saying that. Here's the irony: I don't feel unseen in that way. And that's a big word. Broadly speaking, I don't feel underappreciated. I feel appreciated. But certainly there have been episodes of not being seen along the way, and there continue to be episodes.

I'll give you an example. The Academy chose not to "see" my work in *Da 5 Bloods*. And I'm saying "see" in quotes. BAFTA [the British Academy of Film and Television Arts], the British version of the Academy, chose not to "see" my work. The Golden Globes chose not to "see" my work as an actor. The SAG [Screen Actors Guild] Awards chose not to "see" my work.

BLVR: But the public saw the work, and deemed it work that needed to be recognized by all those institutions. And as we sit here, we're putting quotes around the ability of those institutions to "see," because they're not particularly your audience. They are *an* audience, but they're also involved in and attuned to those methods you mentioned that may suppress, control, and contain.

DL: Yes, I have a relationship, whether or not I want to, with those "institutions." Because I work in Hollywood, I work inside that construct. So, look, I don't want to harp on that. I raise that just as an example of not being "seen."

BLVR: I remember, in one of the first phone conversations we ever had, you were in Oakland at a grocery store. And as you were making your way to the checkout line, a woman stopped you—a Black woman, a Black American. She saw you and she said, "I know you." In all her excitement and love, she began gushing about the roles she'd seen you in. That moment reminded me of bumping into someone you did not expect to see at a family reunion, and then tracing back the ways you're related. There was a kind of claiming—she was claiming you.

DL: Yes, and you asked me, *What does it mean to be seen?* It means everything, particularly in the context of those areas of the industry that do not "see" me. So, on some level, my salvation is within myself—the ability, the capability, the will I have to continue working. And it also resides in my audiences: people like yourself, the woman in the grocery store, the people in the British Library this afternoon. It resides there.

BLVR: I cannot help but think of stopping by Peckham Hill to see the large-scale murals of Black British actors.[4] You were standing near your portrait and a young brother walked by and said, "I see you."

There were several encounters with folks who stopped to talk with you about your work, people of all walks of life who recognized you—who *saw* you. I am remembering in particular, as we were leaving Peckham Hill, the young British Caribbean woman, an aspiring actress, who stopped to talk and who knew the very hospital you were born in. That's how much you mean to these audiences as well.

DL: And that means the world to me. I made a little joke—I think I said something flip. But yes, she knew that.

BLVR: She knew that. It meant something to her. It told her something about herself.

DL: Yes. That's exactly right. ✯

4. This is a series of striking sepia portraits, by photographer Franklyn Rodgers and conceptualized by Fraser James's organization Underexposed Arts, that includes David Oyelowo, Marianne Jean-Baptiste, and Idris Elba.

MICROINTERVIEW WITH DUSTIN PAYSEUR, PART V

THE BELIEVER: The new record, *Bunny*, feels like a return to minimalism after the maximalism of the preceding record, *Somersault*. How has this paring back opened up new possibilities in your songwriting?

DUSTIN PAYSEUR: With *Somersault*, I wanted to prove that I could do more than write simple, minimal songs. So I was like, All right, I'm gonna go really big. I made a huge checklist of instruments I wanted to go on the record: harpsichord, pedal steel, saxophone. Everything's going on this record—I'm going for *Pet Sounds*. [*Laughs*] And it was a fun challenge. But I didn't want to go too far in that direction. I don't think experimenting on a particular record should entirely change a band's sound. Many times you see bands slowly change their sound to be a more and more extreme version of that one record they put out early on, which can be cool. Like the Beatles just kept getting more and more psychedelic; My Bloody Valentine kept getting louder. I think that's neat, but I also think you should just go totally blank canvas with each new record. *Bunny* was a palate cleanser in a way. ✯

THE MAKING OF THE BURU QUARTET

HOW PRAMOEDYA ANANTA TOER, INDONESIA'S PREEMINENT NOVELIST, MANAGED TO COMPOSE HIS MASTERPIECE WHILE EXILED ON A REMOTE PRISON ISLAND

BY JOEL WHITNEY

Buru Island
prison camp
Spoken 1973
Written 1975

DISCUSSED: *Buru Island Humanitarian Project, The Throb of Injustice, The Cold War, An Unforgiving Tropical Sun, Non-Aligned Solidarity, Tariq Ali, This Earth of Mankind, Literary Vows, New Order, Wide-Blade Parangs, Sukarno, Ad Hoc Militias, The River Brantas, Spice Islands, Adri XV, Java Sea, Oei Hiem Hwie, Eastern Star, Social Realism, Torture Hut, A Saga of Interrogations, Lekra, Hidden Notebooks, Clove Cigarettes, Shadow Puppet Master, Kartini, Collective Histories, Mochtar Lubis, Utilization, Jean-Paul Sartre's Typewriter, Corvée, Banana Leaves, Ex-Tapols, Tanjung Pandan, Hands of Friendship, Uniformed Apparatchiks, Richard Oh, Xeroxed Samizdat*

ILLUSTRATIONS BY:
Kristian Hammerstad

100 YEARS OF PRAMOEDYA

On October 6, 1973, Pramoedya Ananta Toer was ordered by prison guards to run double-time across Buru Island. The writer had been arrested eight years before, taken into custody in the middle of the night. Detained without charges alongside thousands of other men and women, Toer was sent to Buru—a prison island far east of Java and Bali—and forced to toil under the scorching sun. He was desolate, not only because of the Sisyphean labor he was made to perform, the inability to write, and the gnawing feeling of injustice, but also because he was separated from his family. Before prison, he had been happily married to his beloved Maimoenah, his second wife and mother to five of his children. After several years of seclusion from the outside world, Toer was hopeful that the press junket he was being forced to attend could be an opportunity to petition for the freedoms that had been revoked when he was imprisoned, if not ensure his release. It would be the closest he would get to a trial, during which he could publicly question the validity of his arrest.

After crossing dense jungles and shallow rivers, he arrived at the prison camp's headquarters, where journalists and psychologists were waiting. But this was no ordinary debriefing. All who were in attendance were collaborating with the dictatorship of General Suharto, who—like many Indonesians—used only one name. Suharto had come to power in a military coup that happened just before Toer was arrested, and now, thanks to the work of Amnesty International, Buru's political prisoners had become a publicity problem for the regime. After eight years in prison, Toer saw this as his best chance to return to his home in Jakarta and to write. But the journalists didn't appear to care about the injustice of his arrest. They interrupted to ask if, in fact, he might agree that his arrest had been necessary. A year earlier, he had undergone a similar ordeal. But during that prior junket, he had at least been able to curry favor with the journalists.

An old rival, a writer and editor named Mochtar Lubis, emerged among those asking questions. When Lubis—a staunch anticommunist whose views often aligned with the interests of both the regime and the CIA—repeatedly tried to goad him into talking about the events that had led to the military coup of 1965, of which Toer knew nothing, Toer directed the conversation toward more pressing matters, begging Lubis to help him get a dying friend off the island, and demanding measures to ensure he could write his novels again. "Isn't it true you're a Marxist?" the visitors asked, likely following a script the regime had given them. "Why write about remote history and not about the coup?" He was being cornered, which frustrated him.

"What I write about is my choice," he shot back. "I decide what gives me personal satisfaction and... I don't care whether anyone else likes it or not." He launched into a bitter reflection on the lack of democracy in Buru and Indonesia. Yet he knew his infamous irritability could hamper his release, so he made a point of apologizing. During the junket the year before, his anger had spurred the guards to end the conversation.

After the junket, Toer met with the dictator's second-in-command, General Sumitro, who explained that Toer's imprisonment was not meant to last forever—though he would remain on the island for six more years. Arrested at age forty, Toer would ultimately spend a full decade on Buru as part of a fourteen-year ordeal initiated by Cold War allies of the United States to test a form of right-wing authoritarian reeducation. Toer was one of the regime's most prominent guinea pigs.

And yet after his release from Buru in 1979, Toer's fame would grow in tandem with the public's recognition of what he underwent—and accomplished. He told interviewers about his struggle to write in what he called a "concentration camp" on a sweltering island, where, along with more than fourteen thousand other prisoners, he nearly starved while being forced to farm the infertile soil. Toer was prohibited even from writing letters to his wife and children, though he refused to submit to the ban. Knowing beatings awaited, and that his pages would be confiscated and destroyed, he disobeyed by writing in secret, pretending to adhere to the strict rules, while advocating publicly for his freedom to write. What he said little about, even after release, was *how* he kept writing.

In his first year on Buru, he watched friends get beaten or killed for possessing contraband, or, at other times, solely for the guards' cruel pleasure. He worked building roads, felling trees, clearing fields, removing razor-like elephant grass with no gloves, tools, shoes, or hat, under an unforgiving tropical sun. He milled wood; tended livestock; harvested rice; built barracks, mosques, and churches, while he and his comrades were forced to survive by eating snakes, lizards, rats, and even a newborn baby's placenta (which they promptly regurgitated). Amid all this, he found a creative solution for continuing to write in captivity—by reciting his novels aloud, crowdsourcing feedback on their composition, and finally, while removed to an empty attic with a desk and typewriter, putting them on the page.

As his centenary arrives in 2025 and the sixtieth anniversary of his imprisonment on Buru approaches, Toer remains the twentieth century's preeminent—if unsung—persecuted literary hero. For the Buru Quartet, the four novels he wrote while imprisoned, Toer was nominated for the

Nobel Prize and won several prestigious international literary prizes. His writing has been compared to that of Dickens, Camus, and Baldwin. But if you haven't heard of him, it might be because of the side he found himself on during the Cold War. As Indonesia emerged from colonialism under the Dutch, President Sukarno kicked out the World Bank and sought to maintain Indonesia's "nonaligned" solidarity with other poor nations, instead of siding with either of the major blocs. Refusing to align with the West was a clear sign to the United States and the Indonesian military's anticommunists that Sukarno had to go, and Toer happened to be his most famous literary supporter.

Upon Toer's death in 2006, Pakistani British political activist and writer Tariq Ali remarked, "Had Pramoedya Ananta Toer been a Soviet dissident he would have received the Nobel Prize." Today, new work about his life has begun to trickle out, including *Indonesia Out of Exile: How Pramoedya's Buru Quartet Killed a Dictatorship*, a compelling 2022 memoir by his translator Max Lane, and *This Earth of Mankind* (2019), the first in what the screenwriter hopes will be a franchise of Netflix feature films produced in Indonesia adapting the Buru

Quartet. Despite these few exceptions, Toer remains little known in the US, the land that, he knew, collaborated in his torment—a torment that would have silenced many others. Through sheer will, an unfed, embittered, and desperate prisoner, who had made a literary vow long before, somehow ensured that his ideas about freedom and history would be read and that he would have the last word over the enemies who belittled, stole, blocked, banned, and destroyed his work.

"TAKE OFF YOUR MASKS"

On October 1, 1965, Indonesians awoke to news of an overnight coup. Sukarno, the popular independence hero and president, was under house arrest. The anticommunist Suharto, a lackluster general who had previously been disciplined for corruption, took the reins of the world's fifth most populous nation, while in Jakarta, where he and his wife lived in a house they had built together seven years before, Pramoedya Ananta Toer listened to radio accounts of mass arrests. Rumors of mass killings followed. Friends warned him that, as the nation's most famous and outspoken writer, he should consider fleeing. A friend offered his house outside Jakarta, but the radio reported arrests there too. Days later, Toer sent his wife and children to stay with his mother-in-law. Maimoenah had just given birth to a boy, Yudistira. (Toer had three children from his first marriage and five with his second wife—eight altogether.)

Two weeks after the coup, on October 13 around 10:30 p.m., while at home writing, Toer was jarred from his work. Outside, a crowd had gathered at his gate, wielding knives, wearing masks. Piling boulders from a nearby construction site as ammunition and demanding he come out, they used a sarong to catapult a rock against his door, breaking it. Filled with a courage that was perhaps honed during his two previous stints in prison (his first arrest was under the occupying Dutch, for possessing anti-Dutch correspondence; his second was for writing a book defending Chinese immigrants), Toer grabbed a souvenir sword and headed to the gate, determined to face the thugs of the New Order, as the newly ascendant military dictatorship would call itself.

Toer shouted above their voices, "Take off your masks. Then I'll talk to you." Jeers poured out, threats. Some thrusted their wide-blade parangs through the hot air. His heart was racing; he was sweating. Suddenly a burst of automatic gunfire quieted the mob. Toer and the crowd turned to see four or five police officers and soldiers coming down the lane, and the crowd parted to let them through the gate. They were here to take him to safety, a soldier said, though he knew he would be detained. This would be a typical scene in Indonesia, as the aftermath of the coup unraveled.

Relenting, Toer opened the gate and let the soldiers inside. They waited in the front room while he packed for what he hoped would be a short imprisonment, collecting novels he had been writing, his typewriter, some clothes, toiletries, and money for his wife. His brother had been staying there, and he also prepared for prison. With their items packed, Toer and his brother were led to the front gate by two guards. Toer's hands were tied, and a noose was placed around his neck. Still, he begged the guards to protect his library, offering it to the government's care. He was in no position to bargain. Ignoring him, they led him to a military truck parked on the road beyond his gate.

There he watched a soldier let the thugs into the house—it turned out they were in cahoots—and the men who had threatened him from his gate threw his library of documents, books, and research papers, accumulated over many years, into a pile in the yard and lit them on fire. Out at the truck, he protested. But when he begged a soldier a second time to protect his papers, the soldier smashed the butt of his gun into Toer's face. Turning away from the blow, Toer took it on the side of his head. The blow, and others that followed, his translator John McGlynn recalled later, made Toer nearly deaf in his left ear and impaired his hearing in his right.

The unrest had started two weeks earlier, on September 30. Acting against rumors of a Western-backed coup to overthrow the socialist President Sukarno, his colonels had preemptively arrested several generals they believed to be plotting with the US. They planned to drag these traitors before Sukarno, who was briefed the following morning about what had transpired, and was, by all accounts, not involved. For more than a decade, the US had grown alarmed at the size of Indonesia's Communist Party, or PKI, in its Indonesian abbreviation. Apart from China and the USSR, it was the world's largest, with twenty million supporters. Several US-backed operations to overthrow Sukarno, including multiple assassination attempts and a covert CIA bomber whose pilot had crash-landed in the Molucca islands, had ended in failure.

Though the colonels' nighttime arrests on September 30 were meant to protect the president from another such attempt, they backfired, triggering a military coup led by Suharto the following morning. This coup not only targeted those colonels who had committed the nighttime raids, but also expanded to decimate Suharto's enemy, the PKI. Days in, they went as far as placing Sukarno himself under house arrest. Some said General Suharto, who maneuvered adeptly and assumed total power, had been briefed in advance of the colonels' plans on September 30. But if the details remain murky, it is because Suharto's coup stoked chaos and shut down all but the friendliest media outlets, which were then used to hurl blame at an unarmed socialist party. Only later would what actually happened come to light.

Meanwhile, so many people were being arrested—the tally would reach over seven hundred and fifty thousand, according to Amnesty International; one and a half million, according to Toer—that there was a backlog. Trials were mooted; cases took too long to build, paralyzing the judiciary. Thugs like those at Toer's gate—ad hoc militias coordinating with the military—acted at night or in broad daylight. Targeting left-wing intellectuals and activists, they burned down the PKI headquarters and went after those, like Toer, who merely supported President Sukarno. They killed Indonesians of Chinese descent. They killed students. They even arrested or killed religious leaders and nationalists. The US State Department contributed by providing lists of names. The military and Suharto's new official party, Golkar, wiped out the vestiges of Sukarno's most adamant supporters and any opposition to Suharto's factions in the military—the coup was merciless and total in its scope. "The rivers were red with blood," Toer recalled, "but people didn't understand why! The river Brantas was clogged with dead bodies, but… I didn't see it personally, being already in prison." Between two and three million people were killed in the six months that followed the coup, Toer estimated. In Blora, the small city where he was born, Suharto's forces killed three thousand.

Meanwhile, authorities refused to feed the prisoners. Families who visited their loved ones imprisoned on Java, the most crowded of the archipelago's islands, were told to bring food. But the regime's thrift collided with its abuses. Families carrying food to the prisoners on Indonesia's most populous island also meant that the prisons were swarmed with media; the interrogations and torture that were rampant on Java and elsewhere were at risk of being exposed. The new regime needed to get the prisoners out of sight, far from crowded Jakarta. Turning to history, someone remembered the Moluccas.

Occupying the archipelago for nearly four centuries, the Dutch had used the Moluccas—a string of legendary "spice islands" of which Buru Island was a part—to house prisoners, including the nation's future leaders during the fight for independence. Among Indonesia's 17,500 islands, these islands were what lured Europeans, who coveted cloves, nutmeg, mace, and tea tree oil, commodities that could be sold for a 2,500 percent profit. Like its European colonizer had, the Suharto military regime decided it would send its prisoners to one of these remote islands in the archipelago's east. The camp was named the Buru Island Humanitarian Project, an irony that was lost on none but themselves and their patrons abroad.

A CORPSE IN THE RIVER

On August 17, 1969, Toer and eight hundred other prisoners were squeezed onto a decrepit cargo ship named the *Adri XV*, bound for the island of Buru. Over the course of ten days, during which they suffered from seasickness and starvation rations, the ship sputtered across the Java Sea, the Indian Ocean, and the Banda Sea. Before boarding the ship, Toer had promised his daughter Astuti that he would hoist her in his arms upon his release. He had told his wife she could remarry, but he regretted saying this after hearing that she had done so. Arriving in Namlea, the main town on Buru's east coast, Toer watched a clutch of prisoners ordered off the ship, beaten, and told to serve as mess workers to feed the rest. It was a sign of the regime's unpreparedness. With only five of ten barracks built, the men of Unit 3 were forced to sleep in uncomfortably close quarters. Toer's unit comprised largely dissident intellectuals, including Dr. Suprapto, a human rights lawyer; Oei Hiem Hwie, a journalist and ex-member of Parliament; as well as Tumiso, a primary school teacher in a small village—three men Toer befriended during his time there.

The unit's informal surveys during the first days suggested that the island was a bad choice. Buru's soil was rocky and shallow, there were no roads, the forest was dense but had limited fruit and seed stocks, and for half the year, during the time of dry winds, the river was too low to send food or supplies by boat. As the nation's foremost writer, Toer was spared some of the physical torture his fellow prisoners underwent. But the guards treated him with as much inhumanity as any detainee. His fame also ensured he was surveilled relentlessly. Even a short walk found him closely watched.

Miles inland from the coast, lying between a nexus of small rivers and an imposing montane wilderness, Unit 3 held at least one old friend, Hasjim Rachman, the publisher and editor of the daily newspaper *Eastern Star*. As a newspaperman working in the newly established Indonesian language, Rachman provided a daily reminder of the institution-building that the young nation had so quickly achieved. In the daily's culture section, Toer had written a sometimes combative column on history, politics, and postindependence corruption. The military's anticommunist network had veered right in the 1950s, as a result of being flooded with Western cash, and Toer had used his column in *Eastern Star* to defend the president and remind Indonesians of the rampant corruption inherited from the Dutch, the army's covert alliance with the West, and the need to rebuild institutions that had been hobbled by colonialism and Western meddling.

It was during this time of nation-building that Toer had detailed Indonesia's literary tradition of social realism—works depicting the problems of colonial occupation—as key to its independence, earning him a reputation as a firebrand in the service of President Sukarno. From this work emerged a personal vow to tell the story of Indonesian independence in a series of novels. And this had become, creatively speaking, his white whale. It was so ambitious that, by the time he was arrested, he had only begun to research it.

In his early days on Buru, this project was never far from his mind, even as he witnessed countless instances of abuse, large and small. One day he stumbled across a piece of paper, a work contract between the Buru command and the dictatorship that regulated the prisoners' housing. Like so much of what was put on paper to protect them, it had gone ignored. Barracks that should have been built from strong wooden beams on a concrete base were instead made of flimsy leaves of sago palms over a hard dirt floor and encircled by barbed wire. The soldiers pocketed the savings on construction materials. But even the cheap sago palms, a reminder of neglect verging on cruelty by the guards, would eventually play a role in Toer's literary plans.

The prisoners were worked from dawn to dusk. The unit's tasks included building infrastructure and sowing the rice fields that supplied the prisoners with their food. Clearing elephant grass and rattan vines proved to be his least favorite task, and he complained about it in his memoir, *The Mute's Soliloquy*. When he cleared rattan, knots of yellow snakes unspooled near his bare feet like balls of yarn. As he felled trees, the sky filled with fruit bats and flying foxes. And when the sharp grasses cut into his skin, the wounds were easily infected. As rice rations were padded with bulgur before the fields could be sown, Toer's weight plummeted, even lower than it had been under the cruel Japanese occupation during World War II. The bulgur gave him chronic diarrhea. "I became so weak that whenever I had to go to the toilet, and I had to squat… I wouldn't be able to get up again, [and] I had to pull myself up with my hands."

For those who violated the rules, a torture hut on Namlea loomed. Some of Toer's friends who were sent there never returned. Once, he watched a prisoner being chased by a horse-driven cart. After two kilometers, the prisoner grew exhausted and fell, only to be crushed by the cart. In interviews and notes folded into his memoir, he describes much of the abuse as the result of the guards stealing and reselling for profit the fruits of prisoners' labor, food they needed to live and were ordered to grow. There were communal fields for rice and vegetables, but also private gardens and henhouses for smaller groups of prisoners. If they grumbled over a soldier's intrusions, they might be punished.

After mandatory work in the fields, the prisoners also fished for tilapia or hunted wild boars. One prisoner established a fish hatchery to help survive during those first difficult years, and noticed that the fish were disappearing. The guards had been stealing them. When he confronted them, he was shot and killed. Prisoners were shot for other petty offenses. Apart from the Koran and the Bible, all reading materials were banned. After being caught with newspapers, a friend was tied and dragged to headquarters. Two days later, Toer and some others found his corpse bobbing in the river.

In 1971, his second full year on Buru, he witnessed eleven prisoners murdered by guards. The killings continued each year. When guards disapproved of his shabby clothes, Toer, too, was nearly shot and killed. His clothes had unraveled with constant wear, and he had improvised a pair of shorts from plastic sacks. "When the military saw me," he told an interviewer later, "they screamed that I was insulting Eastern culture by wearing such stuff. They were really going to shoot me." But a friend stealthily nudged the butt of the rifle. Toer was sure that "if [he] hadn't been monitored by the international community, [he'd] be dead." Prisoners also died from malnutrition, malaria, and suicide. Witnessing so many deaths made him all the more anxious to complete his series of novels, which had been delayed by his arrest all those years before; the series would ultimately take the prison island's name.

THE CONCUBINE EMERGES

One day in early 1972, Toer was ordered to attend a press junket held at Command Headquarters near Unit 1—the first of his two junkets as a prisoner. The regime had hoped to calm the grumblings of human rights groups by inviting journalists to meet Buru's two most famous prisoners, Toer and the lawyer Suprapto, who were content on Buru, the regime told the visitors. But Toer, unwilling to be used as a puppet, refused to follow the regime's script. Even with his life in the balance, he decided to hijack the junket by reminding the journalists from India, Australia, and the Netherlands—many of whom had not been vetted—how he "used to be free in everything, thinking and talking and doing, but now I am a prisoner." One journalist repeated false reports that the men had been communists when they were arrested in 1965. Had this changed?

"Everything changes," Toer fired back, uncowed. He had hoped to pivot the conversation to forced labor and the ban on his writing. But with soldiers watching, the junket turned out to be merely the latest in a saga of interrogations that repeated the regime's false claims of arresting only violent, insurgent communists. Toer had never been a member of the PKI and liked to describe himself as a nonjoiner. But he had had to defend himself against the charge of communism many times, partly because he had briefly joined Lekra, a cultural organization that put on plays and literary discussions around the archipelago, and some thought it was linked to the PKI. In 1965, as part of a first interrogation he witnessed on Java, pencils had been placed between a young man's fingers, perpendicular to his hands, and were squeezed together if he gave an unsuitable answer.

Now his public cross-examination on Buru, and the throb of injustice from years of such grilling, provoked his indignation, of the kind that had infused his newspaper columns in *Eastern Star*. "If I could write," he told the journalists in response to a question about his life on Buru, "I would write my memoirs. Now it is very hard for me. I lost my freedom, I lost my family, I lost my work. I am a writer. That's all. I want to write. One day I will write. That is my work and my dedication."

His outburst goaded the guards to drag him back to the isolation unit for violations that remained unknown to him. Just as he and Suprapto were being forced to leave, a journalist asked what message he could carry outside on their behalf. Recalling almost being shot over his shabby work clothes, he muttered, "Clothes. We need clothes." As the junket ended, journalists handed him a pen and a notebook, believing he would be able to keep them. That night, after a guard told him that what he'd said to the journalists was dangerous, he burned the writings he'd hidden in his barracks. (He offers this with little context in his memoir, suggesting that even as he complained of the ban on his writing, he sometimes wrote in secret in hidden notebooks. But the fear of punishment briefly overtook his promise to put words down on the page.)

While he waited for the world's response to his plea, he pursued another form of secret novel-writing: oral storytelling. Its advantage was that it left no evidence for which he might be beaten, or worse. One evening, after a long day of forced labor, Toer began to tell his friends a story on the barracks porch of his isolation unit as he chain-smoked clove cigarettes, which the prisoners bartered for eggs in Namlea. The story, a history recounted by his parents, centered on a *nyai*, or a concubine, a symbol of Dutch enslavement. Under the Dutch, a girl

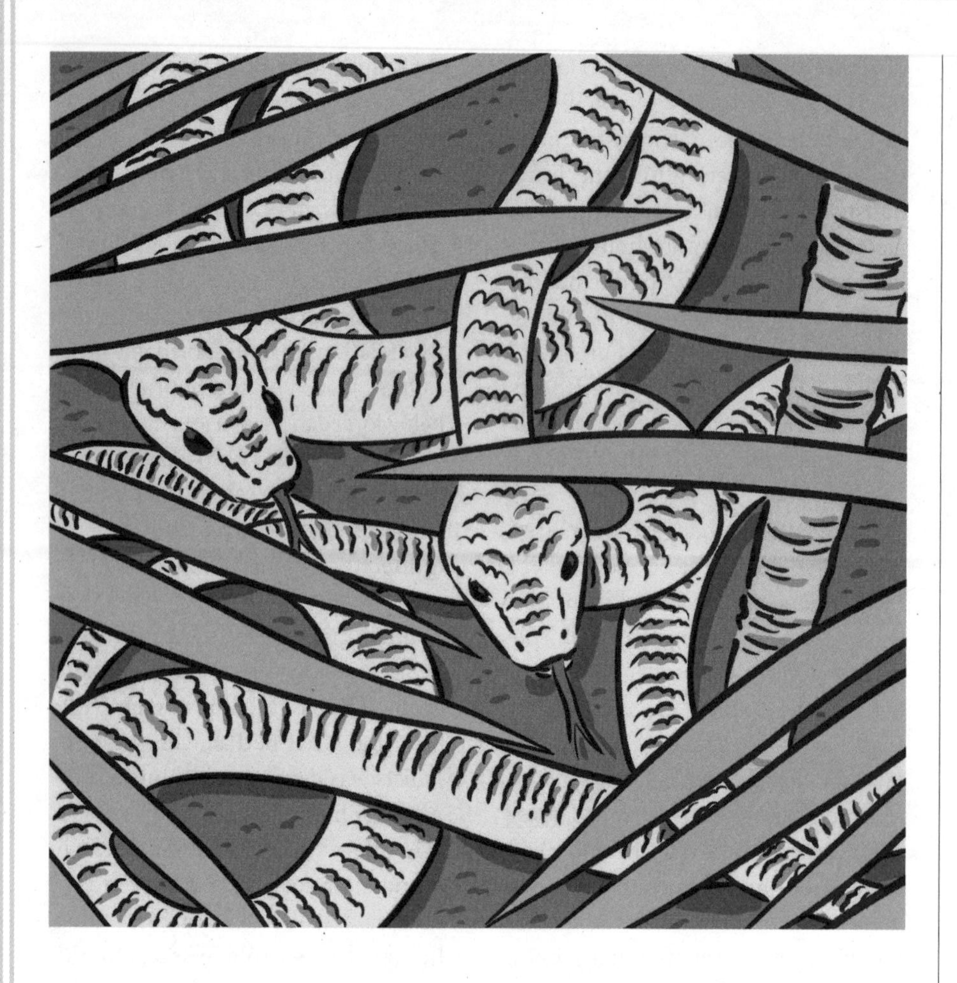

abandoned by her husband or lost in a wager by her destitute father might be sold and forced to serve a Dutch colonial lord. Such was the story of Nyai Ontosoroh. The prisoners considered this a fate worse than theirs. *This Earth of Mankind*, the first novel in the Buru Quartet, unfolds around Nyai Ontosoroh's misfortunes, which begin when her parents sell her to a Dutch sugar plantation owner named Herman Mellema.

As his fellow prisoners rested on the barracks porch, Toer began to weave a historical saga, telling stories the way his mother had before his bedtime. When Toer was a boy, his mother would read him a story each night. But sometimes the tired, overworked matriarch fell asleep before he did, prompting him to pick up the book and read it aloud to himself. The stories he told on the barracks porch were hardly his first stab at fiction, let alone writing fiction in prison. He had begun publishing fiction before age twenty and had honed his work during the two years he was imprisoned by the Dutch. Early novels like *The Girl from the Coast* and *The Fugitive*, which he wrote while he was incarcerated for his part in the independence movement, had won him awards and critical acclaim. Yet here on Buru Island, if he could not write the way he had before, he would do the writing aloud. Later, he would insist that these storytelling sessions were not just about his need to write; they were a way to survive the horrors of his imprisonment. As he told an interviewer later, he "needed to do this in order to encourage the other prisoners to survive, to motivate them with heroic stories about the nyai."

The sessions took place in secret, in an isolation unit where Toer was sent in 1971, two years after arriving on Buru. There, close to Namlea, the prison's commanders could keep a closer eye on him. Among the listeners were his friend and editor Hasjim Rachman, the lawyer Suprapto, and a shadow puppet master—a *dalang*, in Indonesian—whose name has been lost to history. In addition to Nyai Ontosoroh, the stories center around Minke, a student in a Dutch school who initially approves of Dutch and European values. The character of Minke was inspired by Tirto Adhi Soerjo, the first Indonesian to start an anticolonial newspaper in which he advocated for the use of Bahasa Indonesian as the national language. This language, he believed, would promote the cohesion necessary to achieve independence. Here in Buru's isolation unit, Toer dramatized the stories of independence pioneers like Tirto and the feminist writer Kartini—stories he had first heard from his parents. "I don't write to give joy to readers," he once quipped, "but to give them a conscience."

"Occasionally," Rachman recalled in an interview with Toer's translator Max Lane decades later, "people would ask this or that question about what would happen next, but mostly, we all listened in silence, rapt in the story." The nyai story spread across the prison, through Buru's twenty units. Lines of dialogue he invented for his protagonist were repeated verbatim. "Because all of us were suffering," Rachman recalled, "Ontosoroh's words touched us… And the stories did raise our spirits." If Nyai Ontosoroh could endure the Dutch, they thought, they could endure Suharto and Buru.

Nyai Ontosoroh was not the prisoners' only inspiration. They also admired Minke, the privileged native schoolboy who narrates the first three novels of the Quartet. In *This Earth of Mankind*, Minke, who has been raised under the tenets of European culture, falls in love with an Indo-European girl, Annelies, and marries her. Annelies is the daughter of Mellema and Nyai Ontosoroh, who has become his concubine. A vicious drunkard, Mellema spends his time carousing in a brothel, where, one day, a feud breaks out and he is killed. In the trial that follows his death, the nyai learns that under Dutch colonial law, she doesn't hold the right even to guardianship of her daughter. The plantation is given to Mellema's Dutch son in Europe who has never been to the Indies, and Annelies is taken into custody to be sent to Europe. On the day of her departure, Minke watches desolately as his wife is stolen from him, just as she was from her mother. The schoolboy who had once been regaled with stories of European humanism is confronted with the cruelties of Dutch colonial law, and Minke finds himself bitterly disillusioned as he is forcibly separated from his wife. "Only then did I realize how evil the law was," Nyai Ontosoroh tells him. Whispering on the veranda, Toer recounted the story of the courageous concubine who fought the injustice of the theft of her daughter, inspiring Minke to seek out other colonial injustices to fight.

When one Buru prisoner escaped into the canopy and was captured and beaten by the guards, he declared his escape a tribute to Minke. Another prisoner, Muhni, retold the stories of Minke, as did a talented dalang. A prisoner named Eko, Rachman recalled, "went from unit to unit retelling the stories," like a disciple repeating the words of a prophet. These incidents underline the degree to which his fellow prisoners saw themselves in Minke, having struggled against the same European appropriation in the fight for their country's independence just twenty years before. In the prisoners' responses, Toer could see that his stories comforted them amid Buru's heat and misery. But they were also for himself—for he, as much as anyone, also needed the escape, the comic relief. In fact, when asked why he told the stories, he said to Rachman, "Who knows, I might not survive long in Buru. If I die, at least I've told these stories to you."

Another reason for the oration was to invite collaboration. Fellow prisoners gave notes on the impact of his narrative and on its accuracy. In their sighs, laughter, and silences, Toer could hear what rang true and what riled his comrades. Among the items burned on the night of his arrest was a handwritten copy of Tirto's diary; he'd read it only briefly. Recalling it in the prison camp required an act of collective remembering. The writers, lawyers, and historians around Toer helped to fill in the blanks of Tirto's biography and times. Suprapto corrected errors in colonial law. Tumiso, who had become knowledgeable about agrarian law while organizing with farmers in his village, revised the agricultural and labor details. Rachman listened for overall clarity. But this collaboration sometimes made Toer wary. Because of how widely these stories spread, prisoners claimed the narrative as their common heritage, as a morale-boosting collective history. Anticipating that others might claim ownership for what he believed he had authored, he insisted emphatically that the stories were his alone.

THE WRITING ON THE CONCRETE BAGS

In October of 1973, the day before he was ordered to the press junket, Toer dreamed he caught a large fish. As he dragged it to his barracks to share with his unit, he saw that its teeth were made of gold. Dreaming of gold, according to a comrade, was an omen of death. Toer later wondered if this explained what followed, as he would be sent on a several-day ordeal, which involved the harsh junket with journalists like Mochtar Lubis, and written tests that ultimately ended in a forced confession. Designed by psychologists, the tests were intended to gauge his and his comrades' politics, the answers were fed through computers, and each prisoner was ranked according to his willingness to accept the tenets of the dictatorship. Labeled a "die-hard" follower of Sukarno, Toer wound up in the worst group, according to the regime (and its American allies who had helped design the tests).

After the test, Toer was returned to his isolation unit and left in limbo for a few weeks. But with rights groups still grumbling about untried prisoners across the archipelago, he was summoned back to headquarters in early November to read an important letter. Sent by the dictator, the letter vaguely referenced Toer's "mistakes" and suggested that forgiveness, both divine and legal, could be granted if he confessed to his errors. Toer was then ordered to respond. On the page set before him, he wrote that he agreed that forgiveness was key to moving forward—although, stubborn as ever, he did not ask for it explicitly. Still, the letter was a compromise, a confession that would allow the dictatorship to save face in the outside world. *After all*, they could claim, *he confessed*, never mentioning that he was forced to do so.

What followed this second junket, in which his journalist peers mocked him and shrinks talked down to him, was a turning point: Pramoedya Ananta Toer's permission to write was restored. (It is unclear whether this happened because of the confession.) In fact, all the prisoners were newly ordered to perform their vocations: writers began to write again, farmers farmed, singers sang—all work, of course, was meant to be in service of the New Order. The new phase was dubbed Utilization. Others called it propaganda. Toer's life changed drastically.

His new space comprised two rooms on the small upper floor of a cozy administrative house near the Command Headquarters. In contrast to Unit 3 or the isolation barracks in Namlea, his attic office was commodious and peaceful. In a photograph of the exterior taken in the years after the prisoners left, the house appears to be a simple clapboard structure, painted blue and green. A bicycle leans against the front. The grass in the yard is close-cropped, and a eucalyptus tree shades the windows. In an earlier, undated photograph taken while he lived there, the gaunt, long-necked Toer of the first few years has filled out, like a professional fighter training to make weight. His glasses are sturdy, his biceps bulging. Seated at an unkempt desk covered with papers and a typewriter that was rumored to be a gift from Jean-Paul Sartre, he smiles placidly, his hands poised to type. In this space, at last, the first two books of the Buru Quartet found their way from their oral form onto paper. Apart from a typewriter, however, the austere prison certainly did not supply the materials Toer needed to write.

Instead, throughout his imprisonment, a solidarity blossomed between the prisoners. Many who admired Toer joined the project of making his books. Among his informal copy assistants was Oei Hiem Hwie, an acquaintance of Toer's from before their imprisonment, and whose support included manufacturing writing materials, binding the books, and proofing and reproducing his copy. Oei and two other comrades made up a wider solidarity network that brought him food, medicine, and his habitual clove cigarettes.

One day, upon hastening to write down a draft before permission could be rescinded, Toer complained that he had no more paper. Improvising a solution, Oei fetched used concrete-mix bags, which he cut along the seams and sliced into book-sized pages. To obtain a writing instrument, Toer sent a fellow prisoner to Namlea under the guise of selling eggs. This friend left

MICROINTERVIEW WITH DUSTIN PAYSEUR, PART VI

THE BELIEVER: You've mentioned how important it is for bands to stay connected to their roots. How else do you maintain a sense of continuity in your music between releases?

DUSTIN PAYSEUR: I think a lot of bands lose their sound over the years because they just make a fuck ton of money, start playing arenas, and stop listening to cool music. They stop listening to the stuff that inspired them early on. I still love the music I was listening to when I first started writing Beach Fossils songs. I listen to it all the time, and it still inspires me to make new music. I think people get too rich and start listening to other famous people's music because they're friends with them, and they end up with bad taste. It becomes an echo chamber of rich people making boring music. Look what Coldplay has turned into. I used to listen to *Parachutes*. That's a beautiful album. You listen to them now and they just sound like music from a *Minions* movie trailer. ✭

with eggs and returned with a pen for notes and corrections. Toer finally had what he needed to transcribe the novels he had spoken aloud on a tropical porch just two years earlier.

But despite their new "freedom," prisoners still had to perform forced labor—they called it corvée. Under the new arrangement, Toer had to write comic-book propaganda for the regime, as well as development reports based on research they gave him. Cleverly, using this hack work to disguise his real writing—"playing with two books," his friends called it—he worked on his long-dreamed-of Quartet, talking day and night with his invented characters, Minke and Nyai Ontosoroh. It was a tenuous situation: though he could officially write under Utilization, he knew that the guards or their spies could read, confiscate, or destroy his work at any time.

Still, he persisted. His assistants read and retyped each of the pages in septuplicate. Copies were returned with notes from other prisoners. Toer's fact-check was an early form of crowdsourcing, not unlike university peer review. The prisoners' notes commented on all aspects of the story. Poet Banda Harahap wrote in the margins of one page, in awe: "Your narrative and imaginative power is extraordinary, especially because you had to rely on what you remember about the... sources." Toer's imprisonment had morphed into a publishing cooperative.

Though it took months, the saga of how Indonesia fought for its independence came out in a swift, deliberate stream. In early 1975, after less than two years of writing, he completed a draft of *This Earth of Mankind*, or *Bumi Manusia* in Indonesian. The corrections accumulated and the final page landed on the pile. To keep the pages from scattering in Buru's typhoon winds, he bound them into a manuscript using sago palm—which Buru natives ate when food was scarce—as glue. Oei stole a chunk of concrete from a construction site and placed it atop the book to hold the pages together while the sago dried. Finally, Toer wrapped the freshly glued book in banana leaves—the same material used by prisoners to dispose of their shit, so that no one would touch it. But before he did so, he dated the last page:

Buru Island Prison Camp
Spoken, 1973
Written, 1975

5,180 NIGHTS A CAPTIVE

On the night of December 14, 1977, Toer woke to someone knocking. Lighting his lamp, he opened the door and found a prison worker, out of breath. "Your name is on the release list," he said. "You should be ready in case you have to leave tomorrow." Toer received this message with caution, recalling past rumors of release that had gone unfulfilled. It had been painful to indulge in false hope. But in the days that followed, journalists visited more freely, an auspicious sign. One young journalist, Sindhunata, let slip that he had visited Toer's family before coming to Buru. He confirmed for Toer that Maimoenah was still beautiful, and had been selling ice snacks and cakes to make money, and that the children were doing well; his daughter Astuti would go to university soon.

"But do you think my wife and children really want me to come home?" asked Toer.

"Of course they do. They really love you," answered the journalist, his voice breaking. Sindhunata also refuted the idea that Toer's wife had remarried, a lie Toer had been told. In fact, she was waiting for him, he said. "I hope we will not be disappointed again," she wrote in a letter Sindhunata had promised to deliver to Toer. Though officials had initially suggested that Toer would leave with the first group to go home, the reality was that Maimoenah would have to wait two more years for her husband's release. When Toer watched the first fifteen hundred newly freed prisoners sail away, he was happy for them, but disconsolate for himself.

Finally, in 1979, thanks to pressure from Amnesty International and US president Jimmy Carter, who would soon campaign for a second "human rights" presidency, Toer and his cohort of die-hard "Marxist" prisoners were told to pack. But before he—or anyone else, for that matter—could rejoin their families, they were forced to sign two documents. The first included promises never to "spread or propagate Marxist-Leninist communism... upset security, order and political stability... betray the [Indonesian] people and the state... initiate litigation proceedings against nor demand redress from the Indonesian government." The second pledge was an acknowledgment "that they were never tortured and never had to undertake forced labor." With no other choice, Toer signed both.

However, leaving Buru did not mean total and unrestricted freedom. Before his release, Toer learned that he would be subjected to indefinite house arrest under the watchful eye of the regional police. His ID would be marked "ET," for "ex-tapol"—*tapol* being the Indonesian abbreviation for "political prisoner"—and he would not be allowed to publish his writing. Upon arriving in Jakarta, though, he would break each of the conditions of his release.

On November 12, 1979, during the island's seasonal rains, Toer boarded the *Tanjung Pandan*, a decrepit troop ship. After three days at sea, Toer, the schoolteacher Tumiso, and some forty other "die-hards"—who had all failed tests that were supposed to demonstrate their willingness to live happily under authoritarianism—were separated from hundreds of their comrades and sent aboard a small landing craft to Surabaya in East Java. From there they were bused west to the largest military base in Central Java and checked for contraband.

Like others, Toer carried his clothes in a sack, along with his exercise mat and prayer mat. He was searched—his manuscripts had already been confiscated by Buru's prison guards before he left—and he made it through. As the line crawled forward, Tumiso collapsed. Upon reaching the guard post, he told the guards he was sick, and they called him a filthy communist coward. At the next checkpoint, the affable farmer fell again, until he reached Semarang, where, again, he faltered. In fact, Tumiso was being strategic and intentional: Each time he stumbled, the guards, distracted by the ensuing chaos, would fail to check his rucksack, which contained the manuscripts that would become the Buru Quartet. Tumiso's sickness was a ploy to protect the famous Pramoedya Ananta Toer's writings.

Six weeks after leaving Buru, both Tumiso and Toer were released. When Toer's family came to escort him home, he was confused by their faces, having spent 5,180 nights as a captive. Merely an image in Toer's mind for the past fourteen years, Maimoenah finally stood before him in the flesh. It was just as the young journalist Sindhunata had said: she was still beautiful, and he was relieved to see the old love in her face, a love he'd feared was gone. Beside her was a young woman he did not recognize, who shouted, "Papa, papa!" He remained mute and unable to move. Again, she shouted, "Father!" He gasped, realizing at last who was calling him: Astuti! When he had been taken away to Buru, Astuti, his fourth child, had been twelve years old. Now she was twenty-three. The faces of his children, which had been frozen in time on the island, had morphed into those of young adults.

Still dazed, he hugged them. Long ago, he had promised Astuti he would lift her upon his release. She was much bigger now. But he was in good shape. "Feeling strong?" she asked him. He nodded and stepped toward her.

A BANNED BESTSELLER

In early 1980, weeks after his release, Tumiso traveled to Jakarta and handed Toer the contents of his rucksack: one of six copies of *This Earth of Mankind* and its sequel, *Child of All Nations*, the documents he had feigned an illness to protect. In case Tumiso's copies were apprehended, though, five other prisoners and a priest had also smuggled out copies. Among them was the editor Hasjim Rachman and a Catholic priest on Buru named Roovink. Just months after their release, Rachman, Toer, and another

---

MICROINTERVIEW WITH DUSTIN PAYSEUR, PART VII

THE BELIEVER: There was a distinct energy to the 2000s indie scene in New York City, when Beach Fossils was forming. What were some of the defining features of that era, and how did they shape your early work?

DUSTIN PAYSEUR: There was some cool stuff going on that was inspiring to me at the time: Vivian Girls, Crystal Stilts, Woods, Blank Dogs. Those were the kind of shows I was going to. They were part of this new DIY indie scene that in a lot of ways captured that naive feeling of the '70s and '80s, when punk was transforming into indie. It had a punk energy to it, but the music wasn't super aggressive—it was kind of chill. I loved that environment. But I think that scene was short-lived, and not that many people talk about it today. People talk about indie sleaze, which was happening around that time—but that was its own thing. But weirdly, I feel like that time period in New York is just forgotten in a way. So much of that music—if it were rediscovered, I think people would really like it. ★

former prisoner, named Joesoef Isak, decided to launch a publishing house called Hands of Friendship. Their first book would be *This Earth of Mankind*, which, along with its sequel, had been fully drafted and edited on Buru before Toer and Rachman's December 1979 release. (The third and fourth books had been conceived and outlined on Buru but were finished during the years of Toer's house arrest.)

Upon *This Earth of Mankind*'s release in 1981, the novel shattered national sales records, and within a short time, it was banned. The ban was toothless—at first a mere letter from the government asking Hands of Friendship to halt the book's publication. Rachman and Toer refused to acknowledge the demand. But with the release of the second novel, *Child of All Nations*, the dictator's cohort of uniformed apparatchiks enforced the ban. They raided Java's booksellers, confiscating the novels, and Isak was hauled before the authorities and berated. Their efforts were not entirely effective, as novelist Richard Oh pointed out in an interview. Oh was one of many Indonesians who read the novels in xeroxed samizdat. It thrilled him to read books that had to be tracked down through word of mouth and acquired illicitly. The ban had the opposite of its intended effect: instead of suppressing Toer's tale of collective action to end colonialism, it amplified the Quartet's mysterious power.

Though it was still banned in Indonesia, *This Earth of Mankind* appeared in English in 1992, in Max Lane's translation. Barbara Crossette, who reviewed the novel in *The New York Times*, called it "a lesson in the complex psychology

of colonial life—of both the colonizers and the colonized. There are few one-dimensional 'good' or 'bad' characters here." When the book started winning awards, Toer had to send emissaries to accept them. "Every award for me is important because it means a slap against militarism and fascism in Indonesia," he told an interviewer. He was first nominated for the Nobel Prize in 1986, and though he received several subsequent nominations, he ultimately never won. The most prestigious prizes awarded to him were the Fukuoka Prize from Japan, the Ramon Magsaysay Award from the Philippines, and two PEN Awards from London and New York, including the PEN Freedom to Write Award of 1988.

Awards meant that the Quartet's politics could not be sidestepped. When he won the Magsaysay, his old rival Mochtar Lubis wrote an open letter protesting the choice of a tapol, a former Buru political prisoner, as its recipient. The late president Sukarno's daughter Sukmawati was one of several hundred who signed a letter in support of Toer. Widji Thukul, a poet who would lead protests to topple Suharto as a part of the movement called the Reformasi (the Indonesian word for "reform"), also signed. Like Thukul, many of the Reformasi's leaders, who demonstrated to end Suharto's dictatorship and usher in democracy, were inspired by the Buru Quartet.

Reformasi activist Budiman Sudjatmiko credits the great saga written in the labor camp for "opening our eyes" and helping activists imagine how a "global perspective was planted in the youth at that time." Especially important to the student activists was the portrayal in the final novel, *House of Glass*, of the secret police agent who arrests Minke and drags him off to the Moluccas. The Quartet's depiction of the fissures that could weaken democratic movements showed the activists that they needed to band together in a broader coalition. This was vital in the months leading to the birth of a new party, the Indonesian Democratic Party, or PRD, Sudjatmiko recalled in a 2022 interview. They would often visit Toer at his house, where they spoke with him about Indonesian historical events before and after independence. "We discussed history, war, culture—and it influenced our oratory." They even took quotes directly from his books.

Of course, some, like Minke, wouldn't live to see the fruit of their labor. Thukul was disappeared by the regime as it clung desperately to power. With Suharto's fall in 1998, the Quartet's significance only grew, even as the ban continued in Indonesia. As Toer struggled to write through his trauma, editing his prison memoir in the mid-1990s, he was simultaneously besieged by a throng of admirers from around the world, including Swedish embassy staffers (whose presence fueled rumors of further Nobel Prize nominations).

In 1999, after his memoir, *The Mute's Soliloquy*, was published in English, Toer was finally free to travel to the United States for a book tour. He arrived at New Jersey's Newark airport wearing a baseball cap, with his wife beside him, and irritable, as his trip overlapped with a short-lived attempt to quit smoking. While in the Empire State, he appeared at the Asia Society and walked out of a performance of Handel's opera *Giulio Cesare* at the Met. His trip coincided with a *New York Times* review of *The Mute's Soliloquy* by Jonathan Rosen, who praised Toer as "remarkable for his ability to give brutal realism a mythic dimension."

Returning to Indonesia, he joined a new political party, the People's Democratic Party, founded in the wake of Suharto's fall, with the purpose of rebuilding Indonesia's democracy from scratch. But publicly, he deferred to the judgments of the younger generation who'd founded the party, indicating that his membership was largely symbolic. When pressured to write about his own era—the Quartet ends in the 1920s, when Toer was born—he told friends that the present moment could not yet be expressed as literature. Perhaps he was baffled by the present, which encompassed his confusing release, his house arrest, the fall and aftermath of the dictatorship. The prehistory could be carefully studied and written out much more convincingly than the stifling present.

In early 2006, at eighty-one, he died at home from diabetes and heart disease, smoking clove cigarettes until his final breath. To his muted contentment, he lived to see the Quartet's ban rescinded and Sukarno's daughter Megawati elected president. *This Earth of Mankind*, the first of four films adapted from the Quartet, was released in Indonesia in late 2019. Toer's daughter Astuti was there with his grandchildren to celebrate a film that had been born as stories on a jungle porch, then written down and smuggled out of a labor camp. Still, Americans watching the film on Netflix may remain unaware of what its author had to do to ensure its release. In an interview the year before he died, Toer acknowledged that the United States had played a role not only in Indonesia's coup and thus in the murder of possibly millions of innocent people, but also in his own cruel imprisonment. And yet in other late interviews—between his attacks of bitterness—he admitted that, in the end, prison had fostered his writing; and that between forced labor, hardship, and confinement, he "considered all the oppression to be a game. And I took the challenge." ✯

WRITERS WHO STUDIED STEM IN COLLEGE

- ✯ Isaac Asimov, chemistry
- ✯ Andrea Beaty, biology and computer science
- ✯ Anton Chekhov, medicine
- ✯ Arthur C. Clarke, mathematics and physics
- ✯ S. B. Divya, computation and neural systems
- ✯ Nawal El Saadawi, medicine
- ✯ Diana Gabaldon, zoology
- ✯ Alastair Reynolds, physics and astronomy
- ✯ George Saunders, geophysical engineering
- ✯ Andy Weir, computer science

—list compiled by Dan Gutenberg

SUZANNE SCANLON

[WRITER]

"WRITING ALLOWS THE SPACE FOR SILENCE, TOO, TO HONOR WHAT SHOULDN'T BE SAID."

Writers and texts that thrilled the young Suzanne Scanlon:
RE/Search's Angry Women *anthology*
Karen Finley
Henrik Ibsen's Peer Gynt
Eugène Ionesco

I was first introduced to Suzanne Scanlon at Dixon Place in the Lower East Side of Manhattan over a decade ago, at a now seemingly prescient gathering that Kate Zambreno had assembled in collaboration with Belladonna Collaborative: a reading and conversation examining the intersection of fiction and the essay, with Renee Gladman, Amina Cain, and Danielle Dutton. I'd encountered Scanlon's writing the previous year within the exhilarating but short- lived blog ecosystem teeming with brilliant female writers, of which Scanlon and Zambreno were essential components. In Scanlon's blog,* Repat Blues, *she wrote with an intimacy befitting a personal notebook; and without fully revealing her identity, she posted candid accounts of her reading life, teaching, motherhood, and the messiness of being a self.*

Writing, for Scanlon, is the essential crucible through which the material of life is transformed into art, and in a way that's usually not obscured by the guise of artifice. One senses that, for her, living is a form of research, but also that art and writing are just as essential in informing her life. Scanlon has said she thought of her

Illustration by Kristian Hammerstad

second book, Her 37th Year, an Index, *as a fictional memoir in the same way that her first book of interlinked stories,* Promising Young Women, *published by Dorothy, a publishing project, in 2012, could be considered a nonfiction novel: "Both are constructions. Both take from life, and both invent."*

Her most recent book, Committed: On Meaning and Madwomen, *stands apart from her previous two as a bona fide memoir. Scanlon draws firmly from the realm of her lived experience, taking on unprocessed grief from her childhood—her mother died of breast cancer when she was eight—and viewing this in light of the three years she spent in the New York State Psychiatric Institute (NYSPI) after a suicide attempt at age twenty, only a few months after she'd moved to New York to attend Barnard College. She'd transferred there after a gap year spent in Chicago waitressing and reading rabidly. A few months after her arrival at NYSPI, Scanlon was moved to a long-term ward, where she ended up living for years and leaving just before the ward was defunded and closed. Scanlon examines all this in order to interrogate and understand the systems and constructs she experienced, and within which mental illness was treated but also perpetuated. She writes, too, about the madwomen writers, such as Janet Frame and Virginia Woolf, who acted as beacons and who gave her a reason to believe in writing as a way back to life.*

Scanlon conveys in a few sentences what other writers will dilate on about for pages. There's a profundity to her work, and yet it's never without the acknowledgment that language can fail you, her, anyone, at any moment. Her language rarely fails, perhaps because of this awareness, and because of her adherence to Wittgenstein's proposition "Whereof one cannot speak, thereof one must be silent."

Perhaps it's Scanlon's less read book, Her 37th Year, *that adheres to this best—its narrative unfolds in a nonlinear fashion, through brief entries that provide glimpses into the narrator's life as a wife and young mother approaching forty, whose marriage has acquired a lackluster veneer. Published in 2015, the book should be de rigueur reading for those drawn to the recent spate of books engaging with the subject of aging, divorce, and desire.* Her 37th Year *shares with Miranda July's* All Fours, *especially, a desire to interrogate and subvert the canned societal narratives about women in their forties. In the entry titled "Discourse," Scanlon's narrator declares, "I don't want to write a mommy narrative or a menopause narrative. As Eileen Myles said, 'I want to [be] punk about aging.'"*

That energy—that desire to interrogate and shift the narrative handed to us by society, by our families, that we absorb and often repeat to ourselves as a result—carries throughout Scanlon's books, regardless of their genre. Through one lens or another, Scanlon examines modes of care, loneliness, and selfhood, and actively writes against the desire for resolution. In Scanlon's realm, nothing's static, and we are always returning to the blank page.

—Anne K. Yoder

I. WRITING THE SILENCES

THE BELIEVER: You quote Flannery O'Connor in your memoir, *Committed*, in a chapter that recalls the time surrounding your mother's death, when you were eight: "Anybody who has survived his childhood has enough information about life to last him the rest of his days." It's easy to see how your three books have been seeded from and deal with this initial loss, grief, and depression, and, later, your time spent in a psychiatric ward processing this grief. It's more than enough. I am curious how you view this first loss as a source or impetus for writing?

SUZANNE SCANLON: It took a while for me to think that writing about my experience was a possibility. It felt pretty risky. In childhood there were so many things I wasn't allowed to say; I'm not saying I was neglected or abused, but in every family there are certain things you can't talk about. For me, that just heightened my loneliness and sense of not being understood. I recently heard Diane Seuss, whose father died when she was seven, talking about this. She said, *You don't go through something like facing death and seeing a parent disappear at that age without asking big questions about life and what it means to be alive.* So, inevitably, my writing always went to those places. When I sat down to write, I was drawn to extreme expressions of emotion and heightened psychic difficulty. Because that was what I felt wasn't allowed, and I knew there was truth there. I knew, at some level, that was the proper response to everything I'd been feeling and going through. So it's not surprising. Even though I wish I didn't keep writing about the same thing, it's not surprising that I did. That I do.

BLVR: I think everyone writes the same story again and again. And I know I'm not the first person to say that.

SS: Me too. I always tell my students that.

BLVR: Your work often explores how writing is a way to talk about what can't be said. I'm thinking of how *Promising Young Women* begins. I love its first sentence: "Ever since I heard Don Reakes say that the beauty contestant deserved to be raped by Mike Tyson, I wanted him dead." There is such strength in that, a strength that Lizzie doesn't even recognize within herself. And it's like, yeah, she is saying it. But also she doesn't speak it. She writes it.

SS: Exactly. I was just thinking about how Mike Tyson is in the news again, all these years later, and no one thinks about him in relation to that time. I know now what to do with rage and how it relates to writing, and how to deal with it in my life. But then, that was part of coming out of childhood and adolescence—confronting the unspeakable. Rage was a big part of that. Not just horror and sadness and grief but also anger. In childhood, this world of my experience was closed off, and I wasn't allowed to talk about it. And at the same time, there was all this talk that was so far from what matters and what's real. So many coming-of-age books depict this, like *The Catcher in the Rye* or *Franny and Zooey*. They're based on the awareness of the hypocrisy of society, of how people talk about things but don't talk about things that matter and are full of shit all the time. As a young person having to live in that world—in my family, at least—there's this contrast: not only were we not talking about this, but we were using this false, Hallmark language to pretend. It's so much better to not say anything. Writing allows the space for silence, too, to honor what shouldn't be said. Even if I'm working to try to say it, even if I'm never going to get there.

BLVR: One thing that really struck me in *Promising Young Women*, and throughout your books, is the way that people, frequently men, will project their idea of how a woman should be onto women—especially young, attractive women. Men just say the damnedest things.

SS: Yeah, it's amazing.

BLVR: I was wondering how much of your anger was responding to that type of projection and the assumption that their commentary is wanted or welcome. I feel like it's something that every young woman is aware of.

SS: I think it was a mixture. I had very low self-esteem, and I was very ugly to myself. I had buckteeth and no boys were interested in me in high school. So on some level, I wanted male attention. I wanted to be pretty and whatever that offered. But there's the flip side. It also can be a trap. It's so funny, and I say this in *Committed*: You don't think it's such a big problem when you're young, because you're on the side of being highly valued—but being seen as young and attractive puts you in this passive position. As you get older you realize this. I was already slightly passive and I took everything too seriously, including what men would say. I was waiting for approval in some ways. It was always fraught, because it's not really how you want yourself affirmed, right? But I got used to looking for affirmation there.

It's just part of becoming a self, but it's all amped up in our culture—and even more now. I'm so glad I'm not young anymore. I see it even with my son. All the selfies, and looking at Instagram, and all the pictures of other beautiful women. Thank god I didn't have that. It was hard enough just to look at magazines, with the constant awareness of not being good enough.

II. "EVEN THOUGH I HAD READING, I NEVER FELT LIKE I HAD AN ESCAPE"

BLVR: I was recently listening to a *Hidden Brain* podcast episode with a guest who had once been an aspiring stand-up comedian and now has a PhD in communications. She was talking about interpretations of art within the context of a personal desire for closure. People who just want to look at art and say *That's pretty* have a greater desire for closure, in comparison with those who are more open to ambiguity, who are also generally more appreciative of conceptual art. There is a real personality divide between these two ways of seeing and being in the world.

SS: That describes the impulse within my family—that the best way to deal is to close it off. But of course, I was so thrilled by art, the theater, and discovering RE/Search's *Angry Women* anthology, which is still a favorite. Discovering Karen Finley and the rage she expressed, that kind of feminist, and second-wave feminism. But more important, the theater, because that is where I developed as a writer, even though I thought I wanted to be an actress.

In my gap year, and then at Barnard, I was reading great literature; I had an early discovery of the theater of the absurd, where the theater can acknowledge this space of silence. It can acknowledge the impossibility of communication. It can have us sit in those places of ambiguity in a way that, to me, is among the most satisfying expressions of art, of what it means to be human. I remember reading *Peer Gynt* in my theater history classes, reading Ibsen, and then reading Ionesco and so on—and realizing that this was an approach to art and those were the kinds of concerns that felt closest to what I wanted in art. My excitement really wasn't about being an actress in those plays, but it was about the world these writers are creating and speaking to.

BLVR: That's a lot. I had a really profound experience reading *The Doll's House* when I was fourteen or fifteen.

SS: Oh, wow.

BLVR: And Nora, was it? She just leaves Torvald.

SS: Yeah, and that dancer. She spins around!

BLVR: Yeah. I thought, This is the best thing. It was so radical.

SS: In theater, more than in my lit classes at the time, it felt more alive. I just hadn't yet discovered the literature that would feel the same way.

BLVR: There wasn't the internet then, and you write about what that was like too. It involved a different way of finding, and of developing taste.

SS: I think about how hard I had to work to become better read. Part of it for me was simply that for so long my conviction was: I'm going to be an actress, I'm going to be in the theater. I thought I was reading obsessively to become an actress, but without realizing that, in doing so, I was reading to become a writer. The training *is* to read that much. To be exposed to those writers was such exciting training. I was lucky to be in a class where a teacher assigned Marguerite Duras's *The Lover*, and it wasn't even a college class.

BLVR: In *Committed*, you write about this time and space in the year before you transferred to Barnard, when you just read and read. The swath of time was spent in an apartment in Chicago, and when you weren't working you were mostly alone, mostly reading. Anyone who becomes a writer comes to reading in their own way, but there's something so profound and identifiable in the way you state this, about "the sacred relationship between a young woman and a book." The aliveness you felt about reading is striking, especially when considered within the context of the isolation and sadness that you then felt in the everyday.

SS: I remember reading about the same kind of thing in Virginia Woolf's biography by Quentin Bell, her nephew. It's really a problematic biography; the Hermione Lee is much better. The most important relationships I had were in what I was reading, because they could fill that emptiness. I will not say it was enough—of course it wasn't—but those relationships expanded my sense of possibility: of who I was, of being human, of what the world could offer, of feeling close to other people without having to actually be close to them.

I do not want to romanticize it, because honestly, at the time, I would never have said that I was lucky, or that I had all this time and space to read. It was miserable. But in retrospect, the reading fed me in a long-term way, more than anything else. I mean, as much as anything else. And in that way, I am lucky.

BLVR: I don't think you've romanticized the experience. Maybe as a reader it's easier to do that. Like, I've talked with friends about going to live in a convent or a monastery just to get away from everything. Which, you know, has its own issues.

SS: It was so hard to live in my head. Even though I had reading, I never felt like I had an escape. Most of the time I felt so trapped in my head, with this self-loathing. I felt like I was wasting time, that I should have been somewhere else, moving forward with my life. It never felt like, I'm doing something now that will feed me for the long run. But on the ward, what else did I have to do? We didn't have computers or phones or the internet. There was a computer in the library. There was a TV, but I had kind of renounced television. There were people to talk to, but you could only talk to them so much. Maybe in hospitals they do take away phones now. I would hope there's some limit, for healing of some kind. I would want that.

In my gap year, when I got serious about reading and discovered the world of Virginia Woolf, I forced myself to be a reader in a new way. I would set timers, like to sit for an hour and just read, because at that time in my life I was not a reader. I had lost that from childhood. I had to retrain myself. Now people have to do the same thing in a much more extreme way because of the internet. I stopped having a TV, even though I was never addicted to television.

I just watched *The End of the Tour* for the first time, about David Foster Wallace. In the movie they bring up his addiction to TV, and how he'd have it in his house, and then he would have to get rid of it because when he watched, he was obsessed and couldn't stop binge-watching awful shows, like *Knots Landing* [*laughs*]—I don't know if it was *Knots Landing*, but whatever it was that he watched. When he talks about it and when he writes about it, it's so prescient. It is creepy listening to him talk about how we're all staring into screens and watching things made by people who don't care about us, right? Who want to sell us things or whatever. And he's talking about TV in the early '90s. It's terrifying because it's so much worse now. We're carrying them around our pockets. It's meant to just take all your time. And it does take my time. It's sickening to me sometimes when I feel like, Oh my god, I'm trapped in this thing. So now I really relate to what he's saying in a way I didn't when he was talking about television.

III. "BEING FORGOTTEN ISN'T THE CRISIS"

BLVR: You moved from New York to work with him—David Foster Wallace.

SS: Yeah.

BLVR: At Illinois State. Was it because you found a connection with his work? And was it in conjunction with leaving acting?

SS: No, I moved to Chicago first. I remember so clearly being in my apartment here in Chicago, getting that *Harper's* [*Magazine*] issue that had [Wallace's short story] "The Depressed Person" in it, and that was it for me. I was still in New York when *Infinite Jest* came out, and a lot of people I knew, young men my age, were obsessed with it, and these were the same guys who were obsessed with Pynchon. I had no interest. I mean, I had just come out of Barnard, I was a feminist, and that was not my thing. It was such a guys' book, and they were all the same kind of guy, and they still are, although now they paint their nails.

BLVR: In your book *Her 37th Year*, there's an entry under "Oblivion" that talks about a teacher.

SS: I forgot about that part. Yeah, that was a reference to DFW.

BLVR: He assigned the essay "Oblivion" by the poet Donald Justice, who writes of turning to art as a spiritual vocation, usually as an adolescent. But then later he implies that the pursuit of an artistic vocation is the promise of oblivion later in life. It strikes me, reading your work, that *vocation* seems like the right word to describe what writing is for you. But writing as leading toward oblivion, being the author's oblivion—that's so weighted, especially in the context of suicide and David Foster Wallace.

SS: That essay was about three older male poets facing their awareness that maybe their work wouldn't be remembered at all, and probably hasn't been. I mean, people still know Donald Justice. With most writers, though, you devote your life to this, and most people aren't read very much. But that's not why you do it, right?

I'm really curious why DFW was obsessed with the essay. Then not long after that, he named his story and his story collection *Oblivion*. So maybe he was aware he was going to die soon, too, or at least was thinking about that. He had so much fame and attention, but there are so many writers for whom it never feels like enough. On a very different, unsexy note than David Foster Wallace: I've become interested in this writer Doris Grumbach. Do you know who she is?

BLVR: No, I don't. I'm curious.

SS: Somehow I happened on her memoir *Fifty Days of Solitude*. She went to a cabin in Maine for fifty days and didn't talk to anyone, cut off all contact. And she wrote this book about it. I just love the book. She's published many novels over the years that I was never really interested in. She seemed like a fuddy-duddy type of writer, but then I was so thrilled by *Fifty Days of Solitude* that I went back and looked at her other books. She started writing the first of these memoirs as she was approaching age seventy. They're very slim, and they're all very much about aging and facing oblivion. She has a spiritual search and a sense of what it is to face oblivion, or death and aging and mortality. And there's a kind of melancholia present, but she's always reading. It's like May Sarton's *Journal of a Solitude*. They knew each other. And in fact, in May Sarton's diaries there's this great moment where she's like, *Doris just sent me her* Fifty Days of Solitude. *It's very interesting, when I've spent years in solitude, that she just spent fifty days.*

BLVR: Competition.

SS: Yeah, about extreme solitude. I think May Sarton always lived alone, and Doris Grumbach had been married, raised four kids with a husband, and then left her husband and had a woman partner the rest of her life. They actually opened a bookstore in Maine, and then they both, in very old age, went to this Quaker retirement community. I like that she was always negotiating how to have such a rich, full life with her family. But she did this also knowing that always she had to return to the blank page and the space of emptiness. And it is actually a vocation, a spiritual act of facing the blank page and starting anew, as if you've never written before. The books about aging are fascinating to me. In the first she's approaching seventy, and she's bemoaning aging and how miserable it is. And a few years later, she writes another one. Two years later, another one. There are ten years of tiny books about facing death. She ends up living to one hundred and four. I love that that's how it played out. To me, that part is much more exciting than her other books. I'm sure I would enjoy the novels, but I'm more interested in reading these spare, diaristic, memoirish books, all so loaded with everything she's reading every day. To me, it's another way of thinking about oblivion as a subject. And unlike with DFW, being forgotten isn't the crisis. She isn't concerned with that.

BLVR: It seems far more Zen. This idea of blankness and beginnings and their cyclical nature.

SS: I think that's how he wanted to be, but he was not like that.

BLVR: It makes me think of *To the Lighthouse* and Mr. Ramsay, who bemoaned how he might not be remembered like Shakespeare. And how he wanted to get to *R*, but he was only at *Q*. That struck me as such a masculine need.

SS: Woolf's father was probably that way, right? The reason I thought of Grumbach is because I pitched my next book as about reading these Doris Grumbach books. For me, at this stage of life, and with this huge transition of now being done with the parenting years—or at least having my life organized around it—I feel a deep engagement with her work.

Writers think about this. People read all those books about death and books written at the end of life, like *When Breath Becomes Air* [by Paul Kalanithi]. They're hugely popular. So people want that news. That's why I'm reading Doris Grumbach—because I want that news of living in that space for so long, of being aware of your mortality and being aware that this could be the end, not imminently, but at this time

---

A PARTIAL LIST OF TERRIBLE ROOMMATES IN BOOKS AND FILMS

★ Frances Halladay, *Frances Ha* by Noah Baumbach and Greta Gerwig
★ Henry Winter, *The Secret History* by Donna Tartt
★ Spike, *Notting Hill* by Roger Michell
★ L, *Second Place* by Rachel Cusk
★ Dewey Finn, *School of Rock* by Richard Linklater
★ Robert Ackley, *The Catcher in the Rye* by J. D. Salinger
★ Gil and Brynn, *Bridesmaids* by Paul Feig
★ Hedra Carlson, *Single White Female* by Barbet Schroeder
★ Hannah, *The Idiot* by Elif Batuman
★ Alma and Elisabet, *Persona* by Ingmar Bergman
★ Oscar Madison, *The Odd Couple* by Neil Simon

—list compiled by Lula Konner

of life when you have more years behind you than ahead. I don't know older women who speak so intimately about that, except to always complain about aging or just say how sad it is, which I realize it is.

BLVR: But also, maybe you want to be punk about aging.

SS: Exactly. It's profound. It's a profound experience of life, just like giving birth, or childhood, right? So what are other ways to approach it?

BLVR: Right, when put that way, it seems exciting.

IV. HER FIFTIETH YEAR

BLVR: I've been thinking about your second book, *Her 37th Year*, in the context of the spate of recent divorce books that Parul Sehgal classified in her *New Yorker* essay about Sarah Manguso's *Liars*, "Is the End of Marriage the Beginning of Self-Knowledge?"And having read Miranda July's *All Fours* recently, I think of the landscape it shares with *Her 37th Year* too—the homeostasis of a marriage that lacks desire, and writing about aging but not wanting to focus on menopause and mothering, or, rather, writing about aging and the end of a marriage as a fully sexual being. Your book touches on all these things but it's—I wouldn't say a refraction, but it's not a straightforward, linear narrative. Obviously, that's intentional. But the book, like July's, is a fiction about approaching middle age, and all that comes with it as a woman aging in our society. It makes me want to quote Eileen Myles on resisting this sense of lamentation, and these female narratives that we're given that are so dominant, and say, *It's not over yet!*

SS: It's so dominant and yet everywhere around us there are women living full, thriving lives after forty, after fifty. The mainstream narratives are really stupid and they just persist. I hear it all the time, and I hear it from my young students too. Like, *Oh, she's over thirty*, and I'm just like, *What!?* I get that it's relative, and they've never been thirty before. But it's hammered into us in all directions. You and I have talked about *The Substance* and the fact that Demi Moore's character, Elisabeth Sparkle, is fifty.

BLVR: She's fired from her job hosting an aerobics show by the show's older, male producer on her fiftieth birthday. He's like, *Good riddance*—and she's beautiful!

SS: That part of the movie made no sense to me. But in the last few weeks, I've heard two different stories about women and their fifties. One was in *All Fours*: the father's mother jumped out the window when she turned fifty, because she didn't want to get old. And then a few weeks before that, someone told me about a teacher they had, a Chinese woman who was sick with a chronic illness. Instead of treating it, she decided to go to Switzerland and do assisted suicide, in part because she didn't want to age and she didn't want to deal with losing her looks as she approached fifty. And to both these stories I was like, Damn, this just

BLVR: That's real avoidance.

SS: She broadcast it live. And she made a whole video talking about what she was doing and then broadcast it on social media while everybody was watching. And there's all this chatter about it—people criticizing her, people admiring her. I had to keep saying, Wait! It was because she didn't want to live past fifty? Like, OK. My life past fifty is so much better than my life before fifty, honestly. Not that things were miserable in my thirties and forties, but in many ways—in my headspace, in my awareness, my sense of who I am—it's so nice.

BLVR: You come into yourself.

SS: Yes, to have all these references. I really appreciate you talking about *Her 37th Year*. I feel sad that nobody reads it. I'm happy people are reading *Committed*, and I think it's awesome that people are reading *Promising Young Women*, but also in practical terms, they both have good distribution. It's so frustrating to me, because I am really proud of *Her 37th Year* in a different way, and people just can't buy it, because stores have a hard time stocking it, and it's difficult to find through the usual online retailers.

BLVR: Well, people should order it directly from Noemi [Press] in support.

Because *Her 37th Year* is a badass book about aging, not about refusing aging but really embracing it, and so aware. The narrator has reached some of the milestones she once thought would make her happy, and she's realizing that it's not enough. That no one thing is ever enough. Other desires creep in. It is so real.

SS: I guess this was the divorce book I didn't write. It doesn't end with divorce—but it was.

V. "I WAS TERRIFIED OF THE SIMPLER, EXPECTED ANSWER"

BLVR: Of your three books, *Her 37th Year* is the one steeped in longing and desire. I actually wanted to ask you about the form, because so much of your work utilizes fragmentation. Although there is a different logic to each book. In *Her 37th Year*, there is a very specific abecedarian type of container. Stylistically, I find it suits the sense of movement. I would love to hear you talk about fragmentation and if this modality reflects the ways you process narrative.

SS: I think it doesn't. *Her 37th Year* didn't start with the index. It came with revision. I sometimes try experiments of radical revision, like adding a wild form to a text to see what happens. In some of the stories—like in *Promising Young Women*'s "Constant Observation"—the structure allowed me to almost write mini-chapters within the numbered fragments.

I've taught creative nonfiction over the past many years, and I have read all sorts of essayists, including writers like Maggie Nelson and Claudia Rankine. I found their fragmentation—particularly Maggie Nelson's in *The Argonauts*—very satisfying, because it allows her to jump around but each fragment is so specific. For me, the fragment is one among many types of organizational tricks and frames that help me write.

BLVR: The fragmentation I find in your writing lends it a certain acuity, or sharpness, that serves it well. In reading *Committed*, I sensed that the fragmentation reflected a part of the narrator's experience, in that it reflects a fragmentation of identity and memory and a struggle to build a coherent self.

SS: The worst part about being young is that feeling. It's also great, and it's exciting because everything's possible. But for me the worst part of it was that everything's possible. You have to pick something—and then you lose everything else.

In *Committed*, there are a lot of gaps and jumps—grappling with larger ideas and conceptions about mental illness, and at times coming out of my experience. There were parts I felt I almost had to overwrite, that it wasn't enough to leave the fragment. People bring their own experience and associations and then assume I'm speaking for everyone—and I'm not, you know? It's just such a sensitive topic. So the fragment wasn't going to be the whole thing. But I like the poetic style of the fragment, and I'm glad some sections could work in that way.

BLVR: The impossibility of language isn't as palpable in *Her 37th Year* as it is in *Committed*. Language comes up as this burden, but it's also the medium in which a writer works and creates. I'm curious about your struggles with language. I mean, actually, I don't know if I should be asking a writer about their struggles with language…

MICROINTERVIEW WITH DUSTIN PAYSEUR, PART VIII

THE BELIEVER: What's your sense of the younger music scene in New York City today? Is there still a community that you see as spiritually connected to the scene that existed when Beach Fossils was getting started?

DUSTIN PAYSEUR: What I see people doing around the city is—it's always something like: *How can we mash these two genres together that have never been mashed together?* That's been happening forever; that's kind of what creativity is. People are always combining multiple things from the past. But I think there are a lot of artists right now who are embracing music from the pop world, whereas the bands in the late 2000s and early 2010s were only listening to records that came out decades before. They weren't trying to embrace anything that sounded new or contemporary. But right now a lot of these young artists are blending it all together in a weird way. ★

SS: It's why you're a writer, right? [*Laughs*] That's the role of a writer: someone for whom writing is a problem. I wanted there to be silences to be in *Committed*. There's this genre of mental health narrative, and I felt I was working in it and working against it. Because people have all these expectations, and all the language around mental health and mental illness has been horrifying for me—it's some of the worst language. But that's why I love "The Depressed Person," because that's what DFW's acknowledging there too.

Now we have more language to use and we want to reach people, which is important and necessary, but the language is also so offensive and stupid in so many ways that it creates its own problems. I wanted silences in the book that acknowledge that. I wanted to bring up questions about language and what's missing, the inadequacy of it, without answering them.

And for me, too, the book was about bringing up what it means to have lived this mental health crisis, in this life, as this person who's been called mentally ill, and what it means to introduce that without resolving it for the reader. Without saying, *Well, now she's better.* Some of the book's marketing pushed that. But I spent the last section of the book writing against that.

I hope readers understand that, for me, so much is about what could not be said. Paradoxically, I had to write more in that third section to say what can't be said—in the language that we have available—about mental illness, about chemical imbalance, about before and after, and healing and recovery, the blah, blah, blah—all that. Exhaustively writing that last section was a way to say what I knew I couldn't say, because I was terrified of the simpler, expected answer.

BLVR: Like the desire for closure, the happy ending.

SS: Yeah.

BLVR: You bring up the question—why can't you just say something like, *I need care*, and then receive it? Obviously, we don't have a system for that. But when put that way, it makes me wonder.

SS: I find the artists and young people in my creative writing classes are recognizing that language of care and using it with each other. It happened in a beautiful way in class, where my students often write about their own struggles, and we talk about reading each other's work in terms of care. I don't think that's the default. It has to be built within a community of trust, and that takes a while. What's most accessible is the medical model and its vocabulary. So there's more talk like, *I have a chemical imbalance*, or, *I have to go to the hospital, to the emergency room*. It's not that those things don't save lives, because they do, but it imposes something else onto what is often just part of the experience of being human and what requires human interaction and interdependence and so on.

BLVR: It strikes me that what's happening in your class, this care within a community, echoes what we need to do politically as well. If you're going to the larger political institutions, then you're dealing with the imposition of the institution.

SS: Exactly, as opposed to the local, and reflecting what people's lives are truly like.

BLVR: I suppose it's easy for me to say that it's remarkable that you ended up spending so much time in a psychiatric ward just before it closed, a form of treatment that's now seen as outdated. Toward the end of *Committed*, you describe a time twenty years after your time at NYSPI, when you saw a young doctor at a public clinic in Chicago for prescription refills, and she couldn't believe that you had lived in a state-funded psychiatric institute for so long. That you had experienced that form of medicine.

SS: Right, of care.

BLVR: Of care.

SS: Because it was care. Again, that was also something that felt really important to acknowledge. I think so many people would benefit from what I experienced, and there are ways in which many people need that kind of care and will never get anything like it. ✯

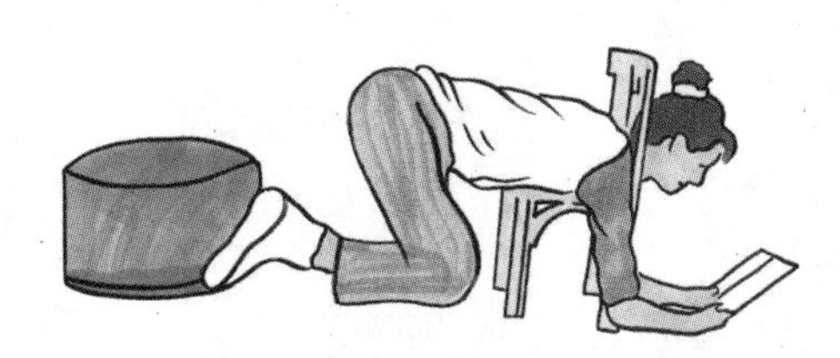

THE MAGI

WELL

CONFRONTING DEATH THROUGH THE EYE OF THE ANIMAL CAM

BY KRISTIN KEANE

DISCUSSED: *Smithsonian Conservation Biology Institute; Front Royal, Virginia; Cheetah Cub Cam; Netscape; World Wide Web; Mangolinkcam.com; Memento Mori; Banquet Ghosts; Stoics; Karl von Frisch; Tschocki the Parrot; Unselfing; Comparative Thanatology; Jackie and Shadow; Waggle Dances; Existential Dread; the Duality of Life and Death; Telepresence; Impressions of Proximity; Mirror Neurons; Murdoch's Kestrel; Spelunker's Frozen Custard & Cavern Burgers*

ILLUSTRATIONS BY:
Kristian Hammerstad

I.

The first image came in black and white: slashes of sable, rosettes, slender legs. Echo's eyes were zipped shut, her face marked with lines as if dripping with tears. Several babies curled up at her belly on the floor of a straw-lined den. I was close enough to their pile of spots that their purrs were audible: their bodies inflated with air and hummed as they exhaled, together forming a symphony of breath. For a brief moment, Echo startled—then they all shifted, jolted awake, tilting their faces toward her with barely opened eyes. Paws pressed against heads as one stretched into a belly-up position, a single leg in the air, its body sandwiched between those of its siblings.

At home, I sat in a dark room nearly three thousand miles away. Outside my window, rain clattered on the deck. I touched the screen of my laptop and counted their heads with my finger: one, two, three, four, five—and Echo—each with a set of paws, a head, tail, eyes, ears. They were being streamed across the Cheetah Cub Cam, operated by the Smithsonian Conservation Biology Institute (SCBI) in Front Royal, Virginia. That first evening I watched for forty-five minutes as they cycled through this pattern of sleep and readjustment. Echo rolled backward, creating a cradle with her body; two cubs lay inside. A pair in the corner embraced. The next day I tuned in and it was more of the same: sleep, stir, wake, rest. By the end of the week I was running the live stream on a separate monitor on my desk, turning toward it when a shuffle of straw indicated movement, or when I paused for a break from whatever task I was working on. I stopped, then looked.

Echo, an eight-year-old cheetah from White Oak Conservation in Florida, gave birth at SCBI in September of 2023 to three male and two female cubs. A few days later, the six were broadcast through SCBI's platform: black-and-white night cams transformed into color at dawn, capturing them as they moved between two dens constructed in the maternity yard where they lived, each rigged with its own cam. These moments were joy-filled and felt oddly mesmerizing, despite the divide between us. I attuned my attention to their movements, and they absorbed me in what felt like an act of magic. Without registering the time, I watched for hours, and while I did, I thought of nothing else.

II.

In 1994, one of the first animal webcams was installed in a forty-gallon aquarium at the Netscape offices in Mountain View, California. Every three to four seconds, it broadcast images of fish to the World Wide Web, a novelty that sparked curiosity and delight. At its peak, one hundred thousand unique visits were made to the FishCam each day. Now an estimated sixteen thousand webcams—streaming from parks, zoos, museums, aquariums, and conservation centers all over the world—provide viewers with live footage of animals. There are so many streams available; reference websites like mangolinkcam.com aggregate these webcams by animal type, directly linking viewers to host sites where they can find exactly what they're looking for. Click on "Aquatic," and links to the California Academy of Sciences, the Aquarium of the Pacific, and the Monterey Bay Aquarium (MBA) appear. Once you're on MBA's live cam site, choose from several subcategories: "Aviary," "Kelp Forest," "Monterey Bay," "Open Sea," "Penguin," "Moon Jelly," "Shark," and "Spider Crab." Visit the "Sea Otter Cam" to view their feeding, handling, and examinations; visit the "Jelly Cam" to observe sea nettles, their umbrella-like bodies pulsing inside the screen's frame before slowly drifting out of view.

Online, in a honeybee hive in Buchloe, Germany, a collective thrums and vibrates. An osprey nest webcam in Charlo, Montana, operated by the Owl Research Institute, focuses on a pair of birds delivering a series of sticks to their nest. The Cape East camera, run by Polar Bears International in Wapusk National Park, pans horizontally across the frozen tundra as it searches for activity on the horizon, spots of brown earth emerging where snow has melted. Sandhill cranes in Gibbon, Nebraska; a puffin burrow on Machias Seal Island; a pair of koalas at the San Diego Zoo. The streams are two-dimensional, plotless, unedited. It became clear in my early days of watching that the magnetic pull I experienced couldn't be attributed to joy alone. The webcams are educational; they steward connections with nature and provide entertainment, and it's possible these aspects contribute to a sense of elation in viewing. But the cheetahs' lives—like those of the other animals—were in most every respect very, very mundane. In the time I spent watching them, they mostly just slept. Despite the monotony, I quietly observed them, sitting on the couch in the evening with the stream playing on my phone as I folded laundry. In looking, I was taken away. *Transported.* Or at least I *thought* I was.

The concept of memento mori, translated from Latin as "remember that you must die," traces as far back as ancient Egypt, and has appeared in different forms. In *Memento Mori: The Art of Contemplating Death to Live a Better Life,* Joanna Ebenstein writes about how skeletons were displayed during feasts, and bronze "banquet ghosts" were passed out as favors to prompt partygoers to savor time. Stoics kept small tokens of death, such as skulls, on their desks, and vanitas oil paintings were filled with time-related symbols that aimed to depict the fleeting nature of life. Smaller memento mori—many of which employed decaying animals such as butterflies, ravens, and snakes as symbols for the death-and-life cycle—were often held close to the body to encourage people to live now, die later, and served as visual cues suggesting that an end comes for us all. The purpose of these tokens was as a kind of aversion therapy and an exercise in placing oneself in the present: meditate on the chosen piece as a reminder of death, and one's fear of the end will dissipate.

Stoics believed this helped one live more fully—that to put death at the center of each waking moment was in fact to be alive. But what if that token were animated instead of static—living and swimming, playing and purring in the space captured by a webcam stream? These technologies can facilitate an appreciation of the natural world, and awe at the diversity of life forms on earth: animals *are* breathtaking, but they are also alive in the present moment, and immediately accessible, thanks to the camera's ability to bridge the distance between us and them. But perhaps more subtly, the webcams also illuminate and sharpen the reality of our own tenuous existence in the material world. We watch not because of the animals' beauty alone, or because of what we learn from watching, but because the webcam—like a memento mori—trains our attention on the now.

III.

Born in Austria in 1886, ethologist Karl von Frisch spent his childhood gathering flora and fauna on the grounds of his parents' mill in Brunnwinkl: moss-covered stones, the remains of a frog carcass coated in debris. He amassed a collection of

MICROINTERVIEW WITH DUSTIN PAYSEUR, PART IX

THE BELIEVER: What do you think about the rise of AI, from a musician's perspective?

DUSTIN PAYSEUR: I think that, as of right now, it's an interesting tool. I got a subscription to Udio [an AI music-generating tool] recently because I wanted to see what it was about. I was putting in obscure post-punk artists who put out maybe like a 7-inch in 1982 or something. But the song that it spits out, you're like, This is crazy—this is good. It's even copying the fidelity of the music and the production techniques. I was kind of shook. It made songs that did make me feel something. I played one for the rest of the guys in the band and it made Jack upset. He was like, "I feel like crying because that song was so good, and I'm really mad that it made me feel an emotion."

BLVR: So, be honest: Did you ask Udio to write a Beach Fossils song?

DP: I did! It made a really bad pop punk song about going to the beach and I was like, OK, I'm safe for now. [*Laughs*] It doesn't know how to make a Beach Fossils song yet. ★

nearly five thousand specimens and more than one hundred live animals, among them his "constant companion," Tschocki, a parakeet. In his autobiography, *A Biologist Remembers*, Karl writes that his father, Anton, a physician, initiated him into the world of looking closely, calling him in after a surgery one afternoon to request that Karl examine an organism under a microscope. Soon Karl was spending "hours between the cliffs, motionless, watching the living things [he] could see on and between the slimy green stones just below the surface of the water." In his observation, he "discovered that miraculous worlds may reveal themselves to a patient observer where the casual passer-by sees nothing at all." Anton encouraged Karl to keep looking.

After a short stint in medical school, Karl abandoned his studies to pursue zoology, and over time he developed an interest in the animal eye. From that point on, he became fascinated with bees. According to his memoir, after he was first "assigned the solitary bees" for study, he observed how different species' nests varied in structure, ranging from simple and geometric to intricate and complex. He found they cast a distractive spell on him; sometimes when he was leaving to go for a walk, he'd get only as far as their hives. Entranced by the bees' interactions, he would sit and observe them instead of venturing out as planned. "I could not tear myself away," he reflects. "The life of the bees is a magic well," he famously writes. "The more one draws from it, the more richly it flows." Karl had found the honeybees' well, tripped, and fell in.

IV.

As the days of cheetah-viewing passed, I spoke about them with increasing frequency: I dropped the cam's weblink into my colleagues' Zoom chat boxes, and spent dinners with friends describing the way they tumbled against one another in the den. When my birthday arrived, my friends enlarged a screenshot image from the Cheetah Cub Cam and fashioned it into a giant greeting card. "Happy birthday to our dearest Keane," it reads. In the image, Echo sleeps in a corner of the den, her toes pointed toward the cam, as her face turns in repose, the five cheetah cubs piled against her, forming a sea of spots.

Irish philosopher Iris Murdoch refers to the transcendent experience I encountered when observing the cheetahs on my screen as "unselfing." In her essay "The Sovereignty of Good Over Other Concepts," Murdoch says that these observed moments of beauty—Echo's spotted pelt, the way the babies nuzzle one another—help shift one's consciousness away from one's own egocentric preoccupations to something outward. Of a somewhat parallel experience of observing a bird outside, she writes, "I am looking out of my window in an anxious and resentful state of mind, oblivious of my surroundings, brooding perhaps on some damage done to my prestige. Then suddenly I observe a hovering kestrel. In a moment everything is altered. The brooding self with its hurt vanity has disappeared. There is nothing now but kestrel." Murdoch's encounter with the bird and mine with the cheetah family result in a similar effect: relief from the self. Breath and fur and wings and claws transport us entirely to the present moment, and become meditative objects, like the Stoics' tokens. As Murdoch sees it, these encounters with nature teleport us away from the backward gaze or future-trips that the Stoics advised us to avoid. Many of us click the links and lean into the screen because that magical feeling created through the eye of the webcam is like traveling to a space outside ourselves; in encountering animals, we gain the ability to shift our consciousness.

Murdoch further suggests in this essay that unselfing is elevated by things that are different *enough* from us, and in a similar vein, the critic John Berger, in his essay "Why Look at Animals," underscores how our interest in observing them stems precisely from these slight adjacencies. We examine them while keenly noting our similarities and differences, but the animals, Berger notes, "may well look at other species in the same way." In Berger's view, animals make no distinction between humans and other living things, and though they resemble us in sentience and mortality, animals lack the ability to "reserve a special look for man"; it's only *we* who recognize those differences, aware of ourselves returning their gaze. According to Berger, this distinction is what maintains our distance from them; "only in death" do our similarities converge. There is evidence demonstrating that some animals *are* in fact aware of death (for example, the study of comparative thanatology has shown that certain animals, such as ants, ravens, chimps, and elephants, are capable of recognizing the deaths of members of their own species). Despite this, we're the only ones who *contemplate* it, according to Susana Monsó, author of *Playing Possum: How Animals Understand Death*. Monsó posits that humans alone have "complex death-related rituals and symbolic representations of death," and are likely the only creatures with "a notion of the inevitability and unpredictability of [it]." We can look at animals, knowing that they're not burdened by the weight of acknowledging—or denying—the end of life, as we are, and that can provide a kind of vicarious relief. Their days, in their routine and boredom, look a lot like our own, but unlike us, they spend their time looking neither too far back nor too far forward. Murdoch writes, "We are anxiety-ridden animals. Our minds are continually active, fabricating an anxious, usually self-preoccupied, often falsifying *veil* which partially conceals the world." Through the webcams, though, a new world emerges.

V.

Karl continued experimenting with honeybees. Poor vision prevented him from serving in the military, so during World War I, he returned to Vienna to volunteer at a short-staffed hospital, where he took a liking to a nurse named Margarethe Mohr. When he persuaded her to help illustrate a project focused on bacteriology, they spent every evening together in the laboratory he had established in the basement of the hospital, and soon fell in love. Shortly after this bright spot formed in Karl's life, however, his father, Anton, fell ill and died. "Those were dark times," he recounts.

Margarethe and Karl married immediately afterward, but during their honeymoon, Karl felt compelled to return to Brunnwinkl, and they cut the trip short. Back at home, Karl returned to the bees. Karl recounts how after his return he became "completely absorbed," falling immediately, "irresistibly under [their] spell."

VI.

In 2024, the Friends of Big Bear Valley's (FOBBV) webcam, which focuses on the nest of a pair of bald eagles, captured the nation's attention. When Jackie and Shadow laid their eggs in January, thousands of people anticipated the start of the new family 145 feet up a Jeffrey pine tree. Viewers like me saw a story of a pair of expectant parents, and watched as they prepared their nest—five feet wide and six feet deep, overlooking the emerald-rimmed shores of Big Bear Lake—occasionally spatting over the placement of sticks and incubation shifts. During one sixty-two-hour period, Jackie went without food, standing guard at the edge of the nest as snow cascaded in and buried her completely. By Leap Day, in late February, Jackie and Shadow's eggs were put on "Pip Watch," the official window of time of their expected hatching. But as the early days of March passed, and the first laid egg surpassed the typical thirty-five-day gestation, viewers began losing hope. The *Los Angeles Times* ran the headline "Big Bear bald eagles' three eggs probably won't hatch: 'Makes my heart hurt.'" Weather, altitude, and nutrition were all suspected reasons why the environmentally sensitive eggs weren't viable, but no definitive explanation was found, only that they wouldn't bear life as planned.

For another month the pair endured harsh weather, continued arranging the long sticks of their nest, and waited. It was hard to observe Jackie and Shadow persisting in caring for their eggs, knowing they had far surpassed their incubation period, yet tens of thousands of people still tuned in each day, realizing that the lives the eggs carried had come to an end. Finally, on March 26, the log recorded by FOBBV moderators stated, “It appears Jackie and Shadow are starting to withdraw from incubation. It usually does not happen momentarily, it is a process. The nest was left seemingly unattended for 15 & 24 min today.” Around two weeks later they wrote: “Jackie spent most of the night on the front porch, a sign that she is letting go. Shadow seems to be more broody at the moment. Hopefully he will eventually take his cues from Jackie.” Four days later—nearly seventy days after the eggs were laid—they lost their structural integrity and collapsed. Why would so many people have kept watching over that long month if underneath all that looking there wasn’t an interest in observing how the birds would face the embryos’ death?

I watched as Shadow stood in the nest, inspecting the eggs’ remains, and I thought of my own mother, who had died four years earlier. I didn’t know what he felt, picking at the remains with what appeared to be puzzlement, perhaps attempting to make sense of what was left in the bed of straw and sticks, but it was familiar to me: What had been in the roost before was now in the past tense. What he had tenderly cared for had been taken entirely out of his present view.

In *The Hour of Our Death: The Classic History of Western Attitudes Toward Death Over the Last One Thousand Years*, historian Philippe Ariès argues that the death toll of World War I changed the way humans acknowledged death in Western society. Where death events were once made into spectacles through memorialization portraits of the deceased, jewelry fashioned from their hair, and grand public displays of mourning, after the war, this pageantry was replaced with a repudiation of death. “Death,” Ariès writes, “has been banished.” He explains how “the tears of the bereaved have become comparable to the excretions of the deceased”; overt attention toward death was newly perceived as a pathology. Extending this idea further, the anthropologist Ernest Becker, author of *The Denial of Death*, argues that we drive ourselves into “blind obliviousness” by distractions like games and tricks and ways of spending our time “far removed from the reality” of what he calls the “terror of death.” He concludes that until we develop a relationship with our own mortality, the refusal to acknowledge our impending demise amounts to existential dread. We fear death, so we deny it; we attempt to transcend it, but rarely confront the details of our own potential ends.

But I wonder if watching animals in savage, wild, and sometimes death-expectant circumstances every day somehow allows us to contemplate death in oblique—and therefore less unsettling—ways. During the COVID pandemic, many people turned to animal webcams to pass the time. A series of online articles promoted their various forms of relief: “15 Animal Live Streams Better Than Anything on Netflix” (*Fodor’s*); “These Wildlife Webcams Will Cure Your Cabin Fever” (*Condé Nast Traveler*); “19 Live Animal Webcams to Get You Through Lockdown” (*Country Living*). Viewers tuned in to follow the animals’ unedited lives: grooming, sleeping, forming webs, and separating fruit from its skin. The redundancy of life sequestered at home had begun taking its toll on people around the world, but the animals went on, unbothered by the simple routines of their days, unaware, as far as we knew, of the tidal shift the virus had wrought on human life. Faced with the staggering death counts in headlines, viewers could toggle to the animals’ oblivion; at times I could feel my own self escaping, and I felt comforted as I watched them eat, groom, and sit. The webcams were signs of life while death was so sharply in focus.

Viewing animals helps us observe the duality of life and death: we can escape from the grip of death's future doom and look without feeling as if we're staring straight into an abyss. The webcam can be the distraction and the confrontation at the same time.

VII.

In the years following his father's passing, Karl threw himself into his study of honeybees; the only time he spent away from work was for Margarethe's birthday. He developed ways to condition the bees and designed special cardboard boxes for their observation; he replaced the sugar water used during honeybee experiments with linden blossoms, then poppies, then roses. He created an elaborate coding system, numbered each bee's abdomen with dots of blue and red paint, and hung white sheets to track their movements as they flew. In a breakthrough that led to a Nobel Prize, Karl discovered that honeybees communicate with waggle dances to show their hive mates the distance and direction of food sources based on the position of the sun. He pioneered the use of video presentations during scientific talks, projecting for the first time animated versions of the honeybees for crowds to view. "The dance of the bees is a fascinating spectacle," he writes, "but one that can never be conveyed by words alone." But more death came Karl's way: of his mother and then of his beloved parrot, Tschocki. He watched the honeybees for thousands of hours and swam deeper into the well.

VIII.

Waiting in line at the grocery store, I watched the cheetah stream. Sometimes in the car I listened only to the sounds of the cam: Echo's trills, the cubs' purrs, or the drum of rain against the plastic flap of their enclosure. I looked at it first thing in the morning, and then again before bed. When I lay awake at night, sometimes I pulled up the feed to watch them sleep, the light from my phone often stirring my husband awake.

"What are you doing, Kristin?" he'd ask softly.

"I'm watching the cheetahs," I'd say, turning over to obscure the screen's light.

One morning I watched as two cubs shivered in one of the dens, their back ends and mantles slick with strips of ice. One huddled in the corner by itself with a tucked tail as it trilled at the others. Echo returned, shivering, with a snow-covered pelt, and the cubs groomed themselves as she churred at another cub visible through the doorway of their den, its straw lining dampened by the cubs' bodies. I watched as if I were there with them, sitting quietly in the corner of the den, but in reality I was three thousand miles away, where the wind outside my window ruffled a neighbor's tree, spreading yellow petals onto the wet concrete.

That feeling of proximity I experienced is created through webcam features that seemingly diminish the distance between viewers and animals. Telepresence—the ability of videos to make things appear closer than they actually are—is in some instances heightened by operators controlling the live cameras. Echo and the cubs were behind a static cam, but they appeared as if they were inches from my eyes, their breaths and the patter of raindrops against the den as audible as if I were inside it with them. Although the collapsed distance is illusory, these close frames create the appearance of a shared atmosphere. In one research study of brown bears in Katmai National Park and Preserve, viewers watching remote webcams had equal or even greater emotional connections to the brown bears than those watching them live in person. Without the illusion of proximity, none of this would have been possible.

When we watch the animals on the webcams, we're together with them in the present tense, despite the discontinuity in space-time, and our mirror neurons help attenuate us to them. In the 1980s, researchers studied the brains of macaque monkeys as they completed certain tasks, and then as they watched their fellow primates complete the same tasks. The scientists noticed that the same neuron fired during both engagements, indicating that the neurons help interpret the actions of others. Also observed in human brains, these neurological "mirrors" help us read what others are doing, predict what they'll do next, and feel empathy toward them in familiar situations. When Jackie and Shadow prepared for their eggs to hatch, or when Echo groomed her babies, we personally identified with those actions and assumed their internal response. When Echo swatted at the cubs' attempts at play, I felt rejection. When Jackie looked at the collapsed eggs, I felt despair.

These moments with the webcams had somehow shaken me out of my constant, trancelike backward glance by thrusting me into the present. They seemed to keep my mother and her death always present, while also reminding me that, whether I liked it or not, my existence without her carried on.

IX.

As I spent more time watching the cheetahs, the memory of my mother's death and the webcam began to intersect. Sometimes I could picture her on the other side of the camera, lying on the straw-covered floor of the cheetah den, staring into the one patch of light cutting into the structure, before she slipped away from me. In my mind's eye, a cheetah entered the enclosure through the plastic flap and obfuscated a part of my mother's body as it lay against her with its coat of spots and molasses-colored nose. As another cub arrived, and then another, they covered her legs and then her arms with their ears and whiskers and long, narrow paws. Her hands and feet and hair slowly became eclipsed by the cheetahs' exhalations and their winding, dark markings. The den filled with breath and movement, but soon it was only the cheetahs'; by the time Echo entered and reclined against her babies, my mother had become buried underneath them: there was nothing left for me to see but the cheetahs and their unmistakable life force.

X.

The winter skies changed to spring skies. Most mornings I tuned in to an empty cheetah den, the creases their bodies made during sleep still visible in the hay. By then the six-month-old cubs were spending more time in their yard, outside the eye of the webcam, and the combination of our time-zone difference and their developmental stage meant I was lucky to catch even a glimpse of them. But one evening as I watched, Echo rested at the enclosure's flap, facing the dark night. The cubs were lying in the corner of the den when one stirred, lifted itself from the floor, moved its body into the corner, and then shifted its face toward the center of the webcam. For the first time I saw both eyes—pupils like dark marbles in circles of white, turned directly toward me. It appeared as if it might step out of the screen into my room, coming so close I could see the wet of its nose. I was closer than I'd ever been to any wild animal, and as I looked into its eyes I was flooded with a feeling of sublimity. I screenshotted a perfect image of its face centered in the frame, peering into the camera.

But when the cub pulled away and I reviewed the image I'd captured, I was reminded of the unidirectionality of the connection. Murdoch's kestrel could look back, but my cheetah couldn't: it observed only the thing recording it—the small light of the camera reflected back in its irises, evidence of our distance. In the picture, the cub appeared to look at me, but the image was really only a representation of my own self making sense of the moment. "Everything around the image is part of its meaning," Berger writes. "Its uniqueness is part of the uniqueness of the single place where it is. Everything around it confirms and consolidates its meaning." It was beautiful to imagine that the cheetahs, whom I'd grown to love, were reflecting the kind of care they showed one another back to me.

But if I was being honest with myself, what had actually captured my attention probably had little to do with the cheetahs themselves. I had managed to use the cheetahs' webcam presence as a way of preventing myself from looking constantly at what death had taken from me. My mother's absence had mangled my life, shoving me into what felt like an inescapable dark hole. But the webcam shifted my attention, and with it I found myself instead in a kind of well where I could swim inside the present—a well with an opening that let the light in.

One morning a week later, I clicked the Cheetah Cub Cam link on my browser's Favorites bar, and in place of the rectangular stream, I found an image of a vulture on a branch against a blue sky. "Page not found," it said. "Sorry we weren't able to come up with anything for that address. Please try one of the buttons below."

The cheetah webcam had been turned off for good, and I could no longer look.

XI.

In von Frisch's final experiment in *A Biologist Remembers*, he tested the honeybees' awareness of time. To do this, he stowed them away on a daylong flight to another time zone to determine whether internal clocks or light patterns were regulating their hunger. Twenty-four hours after their last feeding, he found the bees waiting at their food dish, showing that they possessed their own rhythmic sense of time. Many animals share this awareness that drives them to anticipate meals. Some animals, like crows, can even plan for the future. But as far as we know, they do not wrestle with the concept of time, nor are they plagued by the same worries as we are. They are beautiful. They are good. They do not doomscroll. They do not despair about what is to come. They do not live in the past, swimming in regrets. They are alive in the here and now. For some of us, the webcams are a purely beautiful and silly distraction—but for others, they can give us a chance to see life in a different way, not necessarily because the animals are ultimately so different from us, but because they are not.

XII.

In Virginia in the late spring, Route 522 snakes through miles of green. At the exit for Front Royal, I pass a jiujitsu studio, a Moose Lodge, and a hospice thrift store. Soon lawns, churches, and a long line of people at Spelunker's Frozen Custard & Cavern Burgers appear. Signs of life. The exit for the Smithsonian Conservation Biology Institute is a narrow driveway that I nearly miss: I have come here to stand on the other side of the web camera's eye, and to look instead with my own.

I press my sneakers deeply into a spongy mat filled with sanitizing solution at the gate to the cheetah yards. The lead biologist of SCBI's cheetah care team and a staff member walk me past a trio of males and pairs of females, and I stand at the edge of each yard searching for rosettes in the gold-ribbed grass. Finally, at the end of a long, enclosed lot, I count six heads in the distance. I'm in the same place as they are: Echo's gaze shifts toward us, and then so do those of her five cubs.

When we arrive at the edge of their fenced-in yard, Echo resituates to observe us, and four of the five cubs rise to approach the fence. That feeling in my body—the one I felt the first time I saw them—swiftly resurfaces: a kind of bursting at the seams. They come so close, I could touch them if I put my hand through the fence. They hiss repeatedly, almost in unison, and one cub stutters, making that same birdlike vocalization I heard from Echo the first time I watched her through the Smithsonian webcam. They've grown so much in only a matter of months; they are spectacular in their full spectrum of color. Nothing is between us but the fence.

After several minutes, they recline into a rim of grass, lounge on one another, and roll onto their backs. They take turns stretching against a tree, and I finally see what their life is like off-camera, beyond the four walls of their dens. They lick their paws and groom one another's mantles, and for the first time, they look back at me—*really*, their eyes circles of amber, malar stripes running down their faces as severely as on their mother's. They thump their tails, and when I stand up from my crouched position, they consider me as carefully as I have been considering them for months. I approach to fit the lens of my camera between the barbed wire—and as I do, one comes over to look at me: we lock eyes.

I would like to say that there is shared meaning conveyed between us, that what I feel, the cheetah also feels, but I likely won't ever know this. John Berger writes, "No animal confirms man, either positively or negatively," but we continue to watch the animal cams because behind them is something we recognize as familiar, something that can model for us how to be alive now. "To look," Berger says, "is an act of choice." We look to have our seams burst. We look to explain something about this experience of being human. We look to reach closer to some kind of truth. The cub peers at me, and my well fills: that thing bursting inside *is* magical. In the unfiltered light of day, its eyes are gold coins. I stare into them. The cheetah and I are alive together, breathing into the afternoon. ★

COVER TO COVER

SURVEYING THE COVERS OF GREAT BOOKS AS THEY CHANGE ACROSS TIME AND COUNTRY.
IN THIS ISSUE: *BELOVED* BY TONI MORRISON

Compiled by India Claudy

ESTONIA
Varrak
1997

FRANCE
10/18
1993

FRANCE
10/18
2019

UNITED KINGDOM
Vintage Classics
2023

UNITED STATES
Vintage Classics
2020

UNITED STATES
Plume
1988

SWEDEN
Bonnier Pocket
2014

POLAND
Świat Książki
Date unknown

SPAIN
Ediciones B
1993

UNITED STATES
Alfred A. Knopf
1987

ITALY
Frassinelli
1996

UNITED STATES
Everyman's Library Classics
2006

NETHERLANDS
Nobelprijsbibliotheek
2004

NETHERLANDS
De Bezige Bij
2020

DENMARK
Lindhardt & Ringhof
1993

A REVIEW OF

THE MYSTERIOUS DISAPPEARANCE OF THE MARQUISE OF LORIA

BY JOSÉ DONOSO, TRANSLATED BY MEGAN McDOWELL

"Directly after copulation, the devil's laughter is heard," observed Arthur Schopenhauer, a pessimist about matters sexual and metaphysical, whose theory of suffering stemmed from the impossibility of truly and fully consummating desire. His aphorism describes the condition of postcoital tristesse and avows the futility of life, from which sex only ever offers a transient reprieve. The betrayal of sex, to Schopenhauer, is a metonym for the betrayal of life. We are never finally and decisively released from our desires, and when the frenzied pursuit is over, there is often a sobering reacclimatization to mundane life: all unchanged, unchanged utterly.

But this isn't the sort of revelation that comes to mind for a girl who has had sex just once or twice. It comes with experience—something Blanca Arias, a primally beautiful Latin American arriviste in Madrid, newly unyoked from the supervision of her parents, exuberantly does not have. In its place, she has an unquenchable drive to please her husband-to-be through unconventional and mutinous means. In the opening pages of José Donoso's *The Mysterious Disappearance of the Marquise of Loria*, she entertains a brief and titillating courtship with the marquess—a frill of a human being, and not an attractive one at that. As a lover, he has one thing going for him: a "sinful fantasy life born of exhausting himself night after night in the solitude of his bed at a Catholic boarding school." He invites her to his family's booth at the Royal Theater, where they put on a spectacular display of imagination, audacity, and appetite, stealthily maneuvering their programs for cover as he fingers her to the soaring arias of *Lohengrin*. Everyone thinks the marquess is a "twerp"—an unlikely donee of the feminine attentions paid to him by a lady as handsome as Blanca. The sexual success of this pasty, pubescent boy is the symptom of a "spiritual and moral perversity," a "beautiful and interesting disease"—the strange product of a Spanish aristocracy that might be described the same way Arthur Symons once characterized the Decadent movement in literature.

Publisher: *New Directions* **Page count:** *160* **Price:** *$15.95* **Key quote:** *"Millimeter by millimeter they versed themselves in their mutual topographies so sweaty with fear and desire, the hot vapor of their vegetative hollows, their crevices and protuberances swollen with love."* **Shelve next to:** *Kathy Acker, Georges Bataille, Arthur Rimbaud* **Unscientifically calculated reading time:** *The rebound period for a bereft nineteen-year-old widow*

They get married, but the transgression has dissolved and he can't come. Nature reasserts itself: he dies of diphtheria. Blanca goes into mourning in the prime of her life, while radiating carnal passion and pleasure in black stockings and black ribbons. During this time of contemplation, she looks at her reflection in a pond and concludes that "her own destiny would be to experience everything." Her short-lived marriage has planted a "seed of sensation" that rapaciously puts down roots, blossoms, and bears fruit. She fucks the notary, a compliant retainer who holds the purse strings of the massive wealth she has come into, and who smells like "aged starch or yellowed paper"; she is raped by, then rapes in turn, the count, a sexual connoisseur who is somehow related to the Lorias; she has ravenous sex with a painter, alternately embracing him and devouring his every body part.

This synopsis says something about the novel's content, but the pleasure is in the prose, in the stimulating specificity of Donoso's sexual configurations and the inventiveness of his erotic language, rendered sinuously in this translation by Megan McDowell. Couples don't simply make love but "insinuate" with a "slight push-and-pull," sink into "lagoons of crepuscular water," and become a single "bicephalous and hermaphroditic animal of shared pleasure." Blanca falls in love, but in the painter's absence, discovers she will never really know him. She grows "deathly bored," the last traces of innocence finally evaporating from her. This "definitive and harrowing" boredom is a premonition of something her body grasps before her brain does—that her libidinous romp, momentarily sanctioned for someone else's entertainment, was not the expression of freedom and power she thought it was. Donoso has known this all along—but still he delights in Blanca's innocence, in the precious and evanescent interlude, in the ecstatic moment that begs to be savored before the oppressive order of everyday life prevails again. *—Jasmine Liu*

Illustration by Pete Gamlen

A REVIEW OF

THE HASHISH FILMS OF CUSTOMS OFFICER HENRI ROUSSEAU AND TATYANA JOUKOF SHUFFLES THE CARDS (A NOVEL AGAINST PSICHO-ANALISE)

BY EMIL SZITTYA, TRANSLATED BY W. C. BAMBERGER

According to writer and translator W. C. Bamberger, around 1912 the poet Blaise Cendrars "started a small press, Éditions des Hommes Nouveaux with the help of an anarchist who owned a clandestine printing press at the Mouzaïa Quarter, 19th arrondissement." That anarchist was Emil Szittya, the pseudonym of the writer, critic, and painter Adolf Schenck, whose legacy has largely remained in Cendrars's shadow ever since. His biography bears the telltale marks of a bygone Europe: born to a Jewish family in Budapest, he died in Paris in 1964, having traveled everywhere in between to witness the death of the old order and the birth of a modern, cosmopolitan Europe—as bewildering and miraculous as it was stimulating—a world in which the work of a Jew from Hungary could be "gaped at in the Louvre by tall, thin Englishwomen." On the other hand, Zurich, where Szittya befriended the Dadaists Hugo Ball and Emmy Hennings, was to him forever "a city that smelled of cheese..."

Perhaps best remembered today for his gossipy 1923 book *Kuriositäten-Kabinett* (Curio cabinet), in 1925 Szittya wrote, with *Selbstmörder*, one of the first histories of suicide. A polyglot vagabond like his friend Cendrars, he knew just about everyone worth knowing, and often embellished the truth, claiming to have written books that have since been lost or that never existed—though his fellow hashish enthusiast Walter Benjamin does attest to a missing edition of an early work, *Ecce-Homo-Ulk*, in his essay "Books by the Mentally Ill: From My Collection."

Published in German in 1915—and this year in English by Wakefield Press—*The Hashish Films of Customs Officer Henri Rousseau and Tatyana Joukof Shuffles the Cards (A Novel Against Psicho-Analise)* is Szittya's first extant book. Mixing phenomenological descriptions of mental states and impressions with psychedelic images, it testifies to the narrator's dedication to hallucinations via hashish and opium. As the subtitle implies, Szittya took aim not only at the period's fashionable psychoanalysis but also at traditional narrative itself: his outsize avant-garde ambitions established a now-familiar relationship between linguistic obscurity and literary marginality. (It is no coincidence that *assassin* and *hashish* are etymologically related.) According to art historian Magdolna Gucsa, friends and colleagues such as Hugo Ball referred to him variously as "the knight enshrouded in fog, the pariah dog, the oddball, the satyr or the holy seraph." The narrator's confessions can often apply to the author just as well: "Now I cavort with visions. I have never made concessions to life. It is lovely to be in disguise and to dare to confide in no one."

As often happens in drug-induced reveries, the sentences themselves make sense but the connective tissue between these hashish films often seems to be missing or elided, compounded by the author's unorthodox spelling. As Szittya acknowledges, "I have stolen myself from a film. Now I am strolling along the ocean shore. And I still have not spliced my paragraphs into the proper order." Like in the sordid tales of fellow Hungarian Géza Csáth, author of *Opium and Other Stories*, Szittya's Paris is a province of the demimonde—a midnight city of brothels and sleazy hotels, pimps and prostitutes, a place where boredom blossoms, black tulips frolic, mountains neigh, and blood paints waves of rain. Nonetheless, Szittya manages to complain: "I never have enough images."

Publisher: *Wakefield Press* **Page count:** *80* **Price:** *$13.95* **Key quote:** *"Out of my sadness I paint garish posters for illuminated dilapidated houses. My train has just steamed off with a spring landscape. It is hateful to be a clown."* **Shelve next to:** *Guillaume Apollinaire, Hugo Ball, Blaise Cendrars* **Unscientifically calculated reading time:** *The time it takes streetlight cleaners to cycle through Mark Twain's top hat*

That so little of Szittya's work has been translated into English thus far is not surprising, given the towering legacy of Cendrars, the anti-bourgeois ambivalence of his fiction, and the provocative, sometimes grotesque images he employs—a relic of the casual prickliness of the interwar avant-garde. The effect may be slightly confused, but it is not without its charms and minor epiphanies.

"The world is only beautiful," Szittya insists, "when it has no purpose."

—Daniel Elkind

Illustration by Pete Gamlen

A REVIEW OF

IMMEMORIAL

BY LAUREN MARKHAM

Flying over the snowy peaks of the Swiss Alps, Lauren Markham found herself searching for a word to describe the experience. The ice was melting, and the damage irreversible. "I wanted a space to remember and mourn the vanishing future," she writes in *Immemorial*, her new book-length essay on the climate crisis, memorials, and language.

When I read the book, I had already been thinking a lot about grief and where to place it. My father died in September 2024, but I had mourned him for years before. Like Markham, I asked myself: How do you mourn something you are in the process of losing?

A novice in climate literature, I eagerly took up Markham's text. From within the confines of grief, my mind yearned to go wide, craving insights into the immeasurable problem of environmental catastrophe. Instead, I encountered uncertainty and exploration. In Markham's approach to abstracted loss, I found salves for my own personal grief.

Immemorial takes a loving last look at the dying world. Shores of rotting fish. Extinct birdsong. Fading whistling languages. California fires. Sinking cities. Packed with luminous sentences and piercing examples, from floating islands under California's Bay Bridge to miniature cities made of mud, the text becomes something you want to reach out and touch. The physicality of Markham's language gives shape to that amorphous loss, a temporary holding place for ineffable feelings.

Though it is a slim volume, *Immemorial* catalogs a decades-long conversation between artists, writers, and designers about how to memorialize a declining planet. The book establishes a conduit between private and global grief. Markham sees her grandmother's face in the pale bark of expiring Atlantic white cedars. In a Copenhagen plaza, people hug a hunk of melting glacier "like one might a dying friend."

Markham maintains that how we remember is just as important as what we mourn. "Memorials are the battlegrounds of truth," she writes. Drawing from Maurice Halbwachs's philosophy of memory, she positions collective mourning as a form of critical thinking, a way to reinterpret both the past and the future. She warns against the violence of nostalgia—for a person, for a totalizing national identity, for racialized power—and its whitewashing of oppression. She asks us to think about what we are making as we grieve. As we memorialize, can we form new futures amid the ruins?

These questions gesture toward the tension between permanence and impermanence in memorial rituals. Markham describes a grove of cherry trees planted in East Potomac Park, in Washington, DC, that will eventually be consumed by rising sea levels, a memorial "designed to erase itself." Elsewhere, she considers designer Maya Lin's desire to provide both "a physical and psychic space for feeling" in her work on memorials. I think here of scattering ashes. When we hold the dust of a person whom we loved in our hands, they turn from material to immaterial, but their memory is not lost. Instead, it is briefly resurrected.

When words fail her, Markham documents her climate dread. On an idyllic trip to Mexico, she stumbles upon a shore of bloated fish. All she can do is take pictures. Later, she understands this need to document as "a gesture toward action—something to *do* rather than just something to feel."

Publisher: *Transit Books* **Page count:** *136* **Price:** *$17.95* **Key quote:** *"Memorials are spatial storytelling about the past, but they are also mandates to face the future and attempt its ethical redesign."* **Shelve next to:** *Lacy M. Johnson, Jessica J. Lee, Aisha Sabatini Sloan* **Unscientifically calculated reading time:** *140 Olympic laps*

For Markham, cataloging alleviates the pain of disappearance. In the weeks following my father's death, I relied on film, my own moving memorial. I zoomed in on his wonky smile. I laughed at his obnoxiously loud sniff. I remember the tiny moments that made him my father. In rewatching the film clips, I learned new things about him. I both regained intimacy and acquired insight, a temporary link between myself and my own lost world. "If grief is a condition of estrangement," Markham writes, "ritual is an enactment of relation." Can we perform ritual not to yearn for the past, but to cultivate new connections—with the environment, our communities, and ourselves? Through these gestures of remembering, we can reconfigure the possibilities of grief.

—*Rosa Boshier González*

Illustration by Pete Gamlen

A REVIEW OF

BARBARA

BY JONI MURPHY

Before we consumed movies under duvet-cover mountains or on airplanes flying over oceans, people dressed up to watch them in theaters. Heavy red curtains peeled back to reveal the silver screen as if it were a stage. After the arrival of more-casual movie houses, filmmakers rolled credits over an imposed curtain backdrop; in the first shot of *Frankenstein* (1931), an actor emerges from behind velvet folds to warn the audience that what they are about to see may shock them. Such overt framing devices are less common now that we're used to flipping between reality and fiction.

In *Barbara*, a new novel by Joni Murphy saturated in the aesthetic dream of old Hollywood, this type of set dressing and stage setting is reanimated, with our speaker stoically monologuing her memoir. Her name is Barbara; she is forty years old; the year is 1975. She's an actress filming a Western and having an affair with her younger male costar. In the afterglow of sex she can finally unfold herself, talk to him about the rapes she'd never call rape, the redness of her cheeks after her mother slapped them, and the bandanna she wore over her eyes in a green sedan on the way to an illegal abortion. Now that the curtain's up, she's going to spill her entire life story; what you are about to hear may depress you.

For most of the novel, Barbara's first-person narration stays on a linear track. She whips past the milestones of her family trauma, romantic lows, and career highs, while tapping the touchstones of mid-century pop arts and culture. Barbara's memory of her mother's violence is tangled with her mother's signature smell of "Dove soap and light sweat, Lucky Strikes and L'Air du Temps." On the day she learned that her mother died by suicide, she spent the morning reading Marilyn Monroe's cover story for *Life*. Barbara soon gets out of Colorado and chases the dream in New York City, where getting fingered under the tablecloth in a hotel restaurant leads her to an acting class, which leads her to summer stock theater, which leads her to more roles and more men. Asides like "We discussed atomic weapons and the inspirational Fidel Castro" are time stamps marking how far we have come.

But *Barbara* doesn't read like historical fiction, and real-world events are blips in the story. (Sometimes they are ahistorical, like when Barbara says she observed the day Sylvia Plath died—Plath was famous only posthumously.) Murphy—who studied interwar Germany in her twenties and wrote a master's thesis on Walter Benjamin and childhood—is most interested in the psyche of the woman she created on the page. Yet images are what Barbara's made of. Murphy casts her in many sumptuous scenes: chocolate mousse arriving on a sky-high dessert cart, a hypnotism in Hell's Kitchen, and the great idea to wear "something lacy, bought off the rack from the summer sale section" to your own wedding.

She also employs the trick of some post-*Austerlitz* novelists of embedding photographs within the text. These black-and-white postcard snapshots—mostly open-source from the Library of Congress, plus some of Murphy's own family photos—have the odd effect of making Barbara, whose name was the third most popular choice for baby girls in the year she was born, anyone and no one.

The one thing that characterizes Murphy's Barbara is the sex she has, described early in the book, when she realizes that "a girl can be any object… A girl can be a high arch hidden inside a clean white Ked." The natural blond's opportunistic awareness of her sex appeal culminates in whispered nothings like "Eyes are vaginas." Barbara claims that the best thing she ever did "was marry a man who didn't want to destroy me," though she clearly misses the passion that's part of destruction.

When Barbara muses about how thin she is, or the new bath set she bought from Bloomingdale's, it's clear that Murphy sought to capture a repression so inherent and deep that the woman who's drowning doesn't notice.

—Greta Rainbow

Publisher: *Astra House* **Page count:** *240* **Price:** *$28* **Key quote:** *"The clothing of my memory shifts around, like a skirt twisted so that the zipper's over my hip when it's supposed to be in the back."* **Shelve next to:** *Stephanie LaCava, Nathalie Léger, Joyce Carol Oates* **Unscientifically calculated reading time:** *Several nights spent unsuccessfully scrolling for something to watch on the Criterion Channel*

Illustration by Pete Gamlen

THE PUZZLE OF INCREDIBLY WIDE AND DEEP KNOWLEDGE

IF YOU COMPLETE THIS PUZZLE, YOU ARE A GENERALIST OF BROAD SKILL AND GREAT RENOWN

by Ada Nicolle; edited by Benjamin Tausig

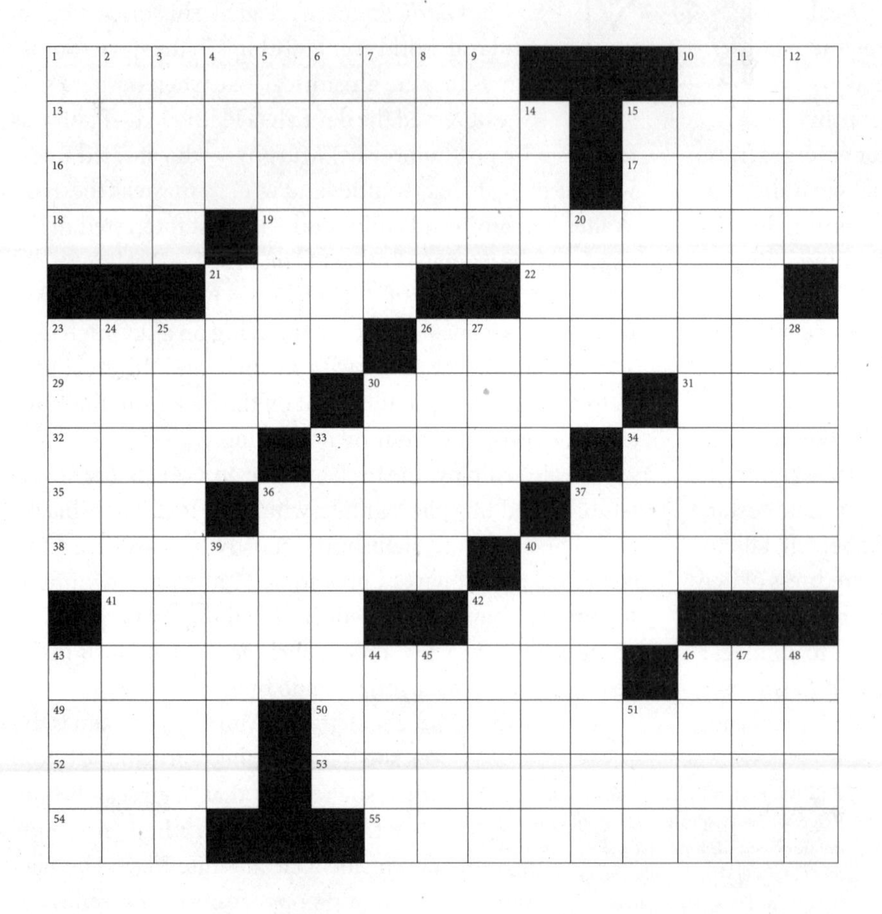

ACROSS

1. Establishment where some fancy people get lifts
10. Where strings are gathered, typically
13. Certain music-industry monopoly
15. Muted
16. "Someone had to say it"
17. Penne ___ vodka
18. Make from scratch, maybe
19. Radioactive element first created in 1994
21. Singh : Sikh men :: ___ : Sikh women
22. "Enchanted" star
23. Actor whose iconic line is quoted at the beginning of Lamar's "Not Like Us"
26. What Guinness World Records adjudicators oversee
29. Muted
30. Bowling ball surface quality
31. Title that reverses to a U.S. government org.
32. "Is it smaller than a ___?" (common Twenty Questions question)
33. Played around (with)
34. Faire offering
35. Disease associated with the Ice Bucket Challenge
36. Converses, e.g.
37. Jarful in a crafts cabinet
38. Forgotten passions
40. ___ sheet
41. Rear
42. Material in a channel
43. What something may be blown to
46. Frequent flier?
49. Activity mentioned derogatorily in "Escape (The Piña Colada Song)"
50. Large pot holders
52. It comes before one
53. Pursued, as the "next big thing"
54. "State of the Union" broadcaster
55. Bassist and former Harvard professor Spalding

DOWN

1. Moved effortlessly
2. More popular alternative to the nickname "Enzedder"
3. Late rapper Artis Leon ___ Jr., aka Coolio
4. N.W.A MC who founded Villain Entertainment
5. Player, e.g.
6. Only watched, say
7. Ostracize, in a way
8. Plus ___ ("nothing left," in French)
9. Cause of harm, legally
10. Rewritten piece of history?
11. Go to show
12. What an athlete might play for
14. Made ineffective
15. First flier of the "jumbo jet," familiarly
20. This place is perfect!
21. The K in Ohio's "KSU"
23. Gross-sounding organs?
24. Best-selling manga series with a talking cat named Luna
25. 1989 musical based on Puccini's "Madama Butterfly"
26. "Now it's ringing a bell"
27. What swingers' clubs should avoid
28. Shared an opinion (with), say
30. Clean sweep's lack?
33. Classical trio, with "The"
34. Apt name for a practitioner of 49-Across?
36. Prom queen's adornment
37. Bohemian beer variety
39. Saturn's largest moon
40. Like the number of entries in this puzzle
42. Clinch
43. Make work with the beat, say
44. Shawarma platter component
45. They're subject to inflation
46. Period of a billion years, in astronomy
47. Santa ___, California
48. ___ noche
51. Papers signed before a large project, maybe: Abbr.

(answers on page 96)

JACKET CAPTCHA

CAN YOU IDENTIFY THESE NINE BOOK COVERS?

CLASSIFIEDS

Believer Classifieds cost $2 per word. They can be placed by emailing classifieds@thebeliever.net. All submissions subject to editorial approval. No results guaranteed.

FOR SALE

BACK ISSUES of *Believer* available (2007–2015)—Destinationbooks.net https://bit.ly/4aJaWL7

EGGERS SILKSCREENS FOR SALE—Dave Eggers has set up a silkscreen studio in the basement below *The Believer*'s offices, and all proceeds from these prints go to help pay the rent for the International Library of Youth Writing. Go to store.mcsweeneys.net to see the wide selection of affordable prints ($90 each), suitable for framing or paper-airplane-making. All of them are limited editions, all signed by Dave. Beautify your home while supporting our new home for books by young writers.

THE INFINITE PLAY—Bathers Library is excited to present the latest in our conceptual artist games series: "The Infinite Play" by Alexandra Pink—an infinitely rearrangeable experimental theater experience for 1–35 players. Find this project and more at batherslibrary.cargo.site.

SERVICES

TEXT YOUR ADDRESS, I'll mail a postcard. 917-412-6791. Brian McMullen.

ART GUY FOR HIRE—Album/book covers, movie posters, & portraits for a modest price. instagram.com/noahjlanders.

WELL WISHES

SENDING LOVE to my dearest Gus as he recovers from a major knee operation. Soon enough you'll be back to tearing across wide-open fields, chasing your favorite red frisbee.

SUBMISSIONS

DEAREST EMERGING AND WELL-ESTABLISHED WRITERS—*Southeast Review* wants your fiction, creative nonfiction, poetry, book reviews, interviews, for our biannual issue. Be weird, be fun, be electric at southeastreview.org.

ON VIEW

COME! VISIT! The World's Largest Collection of the World's Smallest Versions of the World's Largest Things in Lucas, Kansas! Open daily, April through October. Superlative!

NOT YOUR MOTHER'S ART HISTORY—SUPERPOSE is a digital archive and creative studio challenging parameters in the study of art history. With a growing collection of over 500 artworks featuring models of color throughout Western art—from Ancient Greece to the early 20th century—we're building an open-access platform to bring these often-silenced stories to the mainstream. Join us as we redefine history with history. Preview the archive now at super-pose.com.

PUBLICATIONS

(PLEASE) READ hexliterary .com—or die.

HUMOR, DELIVERED DAILY—*Chortle* sends original short humor writing to your inbox every weekday, perfect for fans of *The Believer* or *McSweeney*'s. Essays, lists, comics, and more—all sharp, clever, and irreverent. Subscribe for free at www.chortle.blog.

GLOBAL CHRONICLES: *Voices Around the World* is an anthology of 40 youth stories, compiled by Christine Cai with support from the University of Michigan's Civil Rights Fellowship. In the book, young people discuss topics and experiences important to their lives, such as Thai dancing, bathing in Hungary's thermal waters, India's reservation system, and the importance of a driver's license in immigrant communities.

NEW & RECOMMENDED

HEY, HAVE YOU READ Vauhini Vara's viral essay "Ghosts," first published on this magazine's website? You can now find it in Vara's new book, *Searches*, about how corporate-owned technologies—including the AI model that helped her write "Ghosts"—both serve and exploit our desire for meaning and community.

***HYPOCHONDRIA* BY WILL REES**—Pulling from Franz Kafka, Lauren Berlant, *Seinfeld*, and Rees's own hypochondriac past, this free-wheeling philosophical essay explores the causes—and costs—of our desire for certainty. Author Adam Phillips says this "extraordinary" book "will be an illumination for anyone who has ever wondered if they are ill." Out now from Coach House Books.

NOTHING LIKE THE MYTH—In her debut book, *The Sun Won't Come Out Tomorrow: The Dark History of American Orphanhood*, *Believer* contributor and critic Kristen Martin delivers a searing indictment of America's consistent inability to care for those who need it most. Leslie Jamison calls it "a deeply compassionate, rigorously researched, and passionately argued exploration of the gap between the myths and realities of American orphanhood." Purchase it here: https://tinyurl.com/3paayhre

FELICITATIONS

CONGRATULATIONS to little Pip for all your recent linguistic victories. I especially love it when you say "strawberry," "avocado," and "more rice." It's as if, to you, words themselves are equally as pleasurable as the food they symbolize, and I think that's pretty cool. Can't wait for a life of conversation with you, Auntie

HAPPY BDAY TO THE PANEK TWINS—Next time I'm in town, I'll treat you to unlimited Guinnesses, but for now I leave this note of love. You guys are extraordinary. Xx LB

Illustrations by Tomi Um

NOTES ON OUR CONTRIBUTORS

Aria Aber was born and raised in Germany and now lives in the United States. Her debut poetry collection, *Hard Damage*, won the Raz/Shumaker *Prairie Schooner* Book Prize and a Whiting Award. She is a former Wallace Stegner Fellow at Stanford and graduate student at the University of Southern California, and her writing has appeared in *The New Yorker*, *The New Republic*, *The Yale Review*, *Granta*, and elsewhere. Raised speaking Farsi and German, she writes in her third language, English. She recently joined the faculty of the University of Vermont as an assistant professor of creative writing, and she divides her time between Vermont and Brooklyn, New York. She is the author of the novel *Good Girl* (Hogarth, 2025), which will be translated into six languages.

Daniel Elkind is the author of *Dr. Chizhevsky's Chandelier*, forthcoming from Repeater. He lives in Atlanta.

Chris Gayomali is a writer and editor based in New York City. He publishes the health and wellness newsletter *Heavies*.

Rosa Boshier González's writing has appeared in publications including *Catapult*, *Joyland*, *Guernica*, *Literary Hub*, *Ploughshares*, *The Rumpus*, *Hyperallergic*, *Artforum*, *The New York Times*, the *Los Angeles Review of Books*, *The Guardian*, and *The Washington Post*. She is a recipient of a 2024 Andy Warhol Foundation Arts Writers Grant.

Eskor David Johnson is a writer from Trinidad and Tobago. His debut novel, *Pay As You Go*, was published by McSweeney's in 2023 and was a finalist for the Center for Fiction's First Novel Prize and the New York Public Library Young Lions Fiction Award.

Adalena Kavanagh is a writer and photographer living in Brooklyn, New York. She has published fiction, essays, and interviews in *Epoch* and *Electric Literature*, among other publications. Her photography has been exhibited at the Asian Arts Initiative and at Worthless Studios with Free Film: NYC.

Kristin Keane is the author of *An Encyclopedia of Bending Time* and *Luminaries*. She is a researcher at Stanford University.

Jasmine Liu is a writer living in New York.

J.W. McCormack is the literary editor of *The Baffler* and an ex-poet.

Chris Molnar is a cofounder and the editorial director of Archway Editions. In 2014 he cofounded the Writer's Block, the first independent bookstore in Las Vegas. His first novel, *Heaven's Oblivion*, is forthcoming in 2025.

Szilvia Molnar is the author of the debut novel *The Nursery*, which is forthcoming in ten countries. Her work has appeared in *Stylist*, *Guernica*, *Literary Hub*, *Two Serious Ladies*, *The Buenos Aires Review*, and *Neue Rundschau*. Szilvia is from Budapest, Hungary, and was raised in Sweden. She lives in Austin, Texas, and works as a foreign-rights director for a New York–based literary agency.

Greta Rainbow is a writer and editor living in New York. Her essays, criticism, and reporting on arts and culture have appeared in the *Cleveland Review of Books*, *The Guardian*, the *Los Angeles Review of Books*, and the *New York Review of Architecture*, among other publications.

Jason Schwartzman is an actor and musician. He stars in season four of *Fargo*.

Sam Shelstad is the author of *The Cobra and the Key*, *Citizens of Light*, and *Cop House*. He lives in Toronto.

Christopher Soto is a writer based in Los Angeles . His debut poetry collection, *Diaries of a Terrorist,* was published by Copper Canyon Press. This collection demands the abolition of policing and human caging. In 2022, he was honored with *Them's* Now Award in Literature.

Erica Vital-Lazare is a professor of creative writing and marginalized voices in dystopian literature at the College of Southern Nevada. Her fiction, nonfiction, and poetry appear in *Sojourner*, *Thrice Fiction*, *Callaloo II*, *The Citron Review*, *Literary Hub*, *Michigan Quarterly Review* and *The Baffler*. She is a cofounder of the nonprofit the Obodo Collective and its annual Our Mothers' Gardens Book Festival at Obodo Urban Farm. She is also cohost of the podcast *The Women Who Saved History* and editor of the literary series *Of the Diaspora*, published by McSweeney's.

Ocean Vuong is the author of the new novel *The Emperor of Gladness*, forthcoming in May 2025.

Joel Whitney is the author of *Finks: How the CIA Tricked the World's Best Writers*, which *The New Republic* called "a powerful warning," and *Flights: Radicals on the Run*. He is the recipient of the PEN/Nora Magid Award for Magazine Editing for his work as a founding editor of *Guernica*, as well as the Discovery/*The Nation* Joan Leiman Jacobson Poetry Prize of the Unterberg Poetry Center. His nonfiction has appeared in *The New York Times*, *The Baffler*, the *Boston Review*, *Dissent*, and *Jacobin,* among other outlets.

Simon Wu is a writer and artist. His writing has been published in *The Drift*, *The New Yorker*, and *The Paris Review*. His first book is *Dancing on My Own*. He has two brothers, Nick and Duke, and loves the ocean.

Anne K. Yoder lives in Chicago, where she occasionally dispenses pharmaceuticals. Her novel, *The Enhancers*, was called "a new contemporary standout" among "great books in pharma culture," and was featured in *Wired*, *Vulture*, and elsewhere.

IN THE NEXT ISSUE

Not all contents are guaranteed; replacements will be satisfying

Heartstopper . . . . Shruti Swamy
Reckoning with the alleged abuses of Swami Rama, a widely revered yoga guru, who, upon taking an interest in the author as a young girl, came to define her entire worldview.

Hot, Unlivable Hell . . . . Rafia Zakaria
In Karachi, Pakistan, where climate change and urban sprawl have caused temperatures to soar, procuring water for one's household has become an infuriating daily struggle.

The Last Mastadon . . . . Paul Collins
The short and disastrous life of the world's biggest newspaper.

SOLUTIONS TO THIS ISSUE'S GAMES AND PUZZLES

CROSSWORD

(Page 92)

S	K	I	R	E	S	O	R	T				P	I	T
L	I	V	E	N	A	T	I	O	N		P	A	L	E
I	W	E	N	T	T	H	E	R	E		A	L	L	A
D	I	Y		R	O	E	N	T	G	E	N	I	U	M
			K	A	U	R			A	D	A	M	S	
O	S	M	E	N	T		A	T	T	E	M	P	T	S
F	A	I	N	T		S	H	E	E	N		S	R	I
F	I	S	T		T	O	Y	E	D		M	E	A	D
A	L	S		S	H	O	E	S		P	A	S	T	E
L	O	S	T	A	R	T	S		F	I	T	T	E	D
	R	A	I	S	E			S	I	L	T			
S	M	I	T	H	E	R	E	E	N	S		A	C	E
Y	O	G	A		B	I	G	W	I	N	N	E	R	S
N	O	O	N		S	C	O	U	T	E	D	O	U	T
C	N	N				E	S	P	E	R	A	N	Z	A

JACKET CAPTCHA

(Page 93)

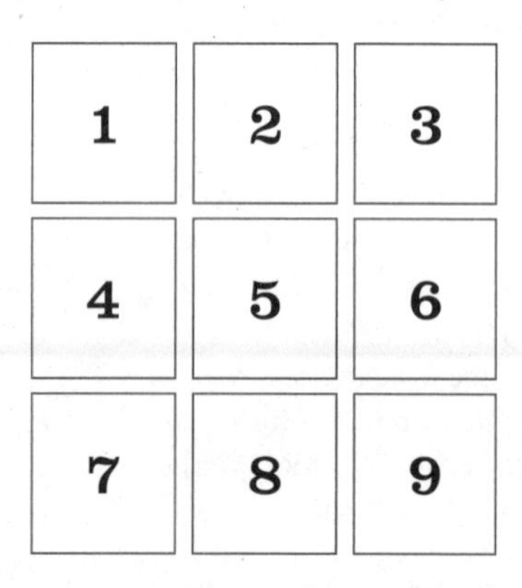

1. *Someone Like Us* by Dinaw Mengestu
2. *Liars* by Sarah Manguso
3. *Vanishing Maps* by Cristina García
4. *Intermezzo* by Sally Rooney
5. *Counterweight* by Djuna
6. *If Beale Street Could Talk* by James Baldwin
7. *The End of August* by Yu Miri
8. *In Tongues* by Thomas Grattan
9. *Small Rain* by Garth Greenwell